The Invisible
WOMEN

Naming and Proclaiming the Forgotten
Women in Scripture and Church Law

SISTER SANDRA MAKOWSKI, SSMN, JCL

WESTBOW
PRESS®
A DIVISION OF THOMAS NELSON
& ZONDERVAN

WestBow Press books may be ordered through booksellers or by contacting:

WestBow Press
A Division of Thomas Nelson & Zondervan
1663 Liberty Drive
Bloomington, IN 47403
www.westbowpress.com
1 (866) 928-1240

Scripture quotations taken from the New American Standard Bible® (NASB), Copyright © 1960, 1962, 1963, 1968, 1971, 1972, 1973, 1975, 1977, 1995 by The Lockman Foundation. Used by permission. www.Lockman.org.

ISBN: 978-1-5127-7956-1 (sc)
ISBN: 978-1-5127-7958-5 (hc)
ISBN: 978-1-5127-7957-8 (e)

Library of Congress Control Number: 2017904153

Print information available on the last page.

WestBow Press rev. date: 03/20/2017

CONTENTS

CHAPTER 1

Setting the Stage—Unnamed and Unnoticed

A. Introduction

> There is neither Jew nor Greek, there is neither slave
> nor free, there is neither male nor female, but we are
> all one in Christ Jesus. (Galatians 3:28)

This is one of the most striking passages in the Bible, and it summarizes very clearly the message Jesus taught from the very beginning of his ministry. All are equal in God's sight, male and female alike. During the time of Jesus's ministry, this was an extraordinary teaching because women often went unnamed and unnoticed. However, as we shall see from further reading of the scriptures, they were named and noticed by Jesus. Jesus recognized women for the gifts and talents they bring to this world of hunger and need. The message is clear, and it needs to be proclaimed and delivered. The message is this: God is the God of both men and women, rich and poor, slave and free, old and young, and God is the God who saves.

But it has not been easy for women, for they have not been invited to participate fully in the ministry of the institutional church. Discrimination abounds because of a patriarchal structure that contradicts the message of Jesus. How is patriarchy defined? Webster defines it with two elements: First, as a system of society or governance in which the father or eldest male is head of the family and descent is traced through the male line. And second, as a system in society or government in which men hold the power. And women are largely excluded from it.[1]

Jesus acted against this patriarchal system. He treated everyone with equal dignity, no matter the gender or class. However, patriarchy has had an enormous effect not only in the choice of scripture readings at Mass but also in many church laws and regulations, which shall also be examined later in this book. There have been attempts by some church documents to rid the laws of discrimination, but it hangs there like a noose nevertheless. There have also been attempts to resolve the issue of sexual imbalance with regard to leadership in the church, and canon 208 of the present code of canon law seeks to protect the rights of all the faithful when it states: "There exists among the Christian faithful a true equality regarding dignity and action by which all cooperate in building up the body of Christ." This is our duty and our call—to promote and practice true equality in building up the body of Christ. We, male and female, are all one in Christ Jesus. We are all sacred in the sight of God.

The following pages will highlight the passages in scripture where women are ignored or misrepresented in the Bible. But it is not because they were not present. For example, Mark does not mention women at the multiplication of the loaves.

The Feeding of the Five Thousand

> When he disembarked and saw the vast crowd, his heart was moved with pity for them, for they were like sheep without a shepherd; and he began to teach them many things. By now it was already late and his disciples approached him and said, "This is a deserted place and it is already very late. Dismiss them so that they can go to the surrounding farms and villages and buy themselves something to eat."

He said to them in reply, "Give them some food yourselves." But they said to him, "Are we to buy two hundred days' wages worth of food and give it to them to eat?" He asked them, "How many loaves do you have? Go and see." And when they had found out they said, "Five loaves and two fish." So he gave orders to have them sit down in groups on the green grass. The people took their places in rows by hundreds and by fifties. Then, taking the five loaves and the two fish and looking up to heaven, he said the blessing, broke the loaves, and gave them to [his] disciples to set before the people; he also divided the two fish among them all. They all ate and were satisfied. And they picked up twelve wicker baskets full of fragments and what was left of the fish. Those who ate [of the loaves] were five thousand men. (Mark 6:34–44)

Matthew's gospel tells the same story, with one main addition in the last verse that changes everything we know about this account: "Those who ate were about five thousand men, not counting women and children" (Matthew 13:21).

If Matthew did not include the phrase "not counting women and children," one would be led to believe that there were no women present at all at the multiplication of the loaves. Yet because of Matthew's inclusion of the phrase *not counting*, we know that women were there. They were just not counted. Because of the culture of Jesus's time, there was a tendency to overlook the presence of those considered less important and omit them from the telling. It is about time that they are named, noticed, and finally counted for their contribution to bravery, steadfastness, leadership, and service in the name of God and goodness.

This book will explore the images used in the Old Testament and the gospels to describe God. Most churchgoers are very familiar with male images of God, but are we just as familiar with the female images of God? Perhaps not. It's time to become aware of the fact that when Jesus uses male images of God, he follows them with female images as well. However, these passages are rarely read to us at the Sunday liturgies. In fact, there is a disproportionate number of passages about the women in the Bible being used at the Sunday or weekday readings at Mass. Many women's experiences and accomplishments have been largely overlooked in the assigned scripture readings. This book will explore some of the significant biblical passages about women that are omitted altogether or are relegated to weekdays, where only small numbers of churchgoers will hear them. It will also explore how many of the passages about women used in church services are actually used to reinforce what some believe to be the weaknesses or proper roles of women.

The concluding chapters of this book will take a closer look at the evolution of the 1917 code of canon law to the present 1983 code of canon law, as well as some quotes from the present Catholic Catechism. It will also recount some of the women missionaries and martyrs who are examples of true bravery and faithfulness. In the end, we are left with the following irony—women have not been invited, but guess what? They showed up anyway. They fill our churches and schools, attend our universities, and work at homeless shelters, at soup kitchens, and in administrative church positions. They serve as lectors, extraordinary ministers of communion, parish council officers, teachers, parish administrators, and canon lawyers. The list is endless. But somehow they didn't get invited into full church positions. Many women in church history have been ignored and forgotten. They discovered that there were many times when wanting to serve or speak freely they were told no. Yet, if one studies the scriptures and reads the words of Jesus, we find that the answer that *he* gave was yes! They were brave and steadfast and spoke truthfully and fearlessly. Many never gave in or gave up. They are role models for us and can give us courage on days when we feel we have no courage left. But it's time to invite them to full participation. The wait is over.

This book will trace the pattern of being unnamed and

unnoticed and will attempt to name and proclaim those left out and forgotten. It will recount the bravery and the call to all of us to be proclaimers of those forgotten and ignored; it will remind us to be the proclaimers of the true message of Jesus.

This book will explore the journey on the path to *yes*. *Yes*, society, as well as the culture of today, recognizes more and more the gifts and contributions women make to the world and to the church. Women have been marginalized for years and now are becoming more and more conscious of their human worth and what they have to offer. On the journey to saying yes, they first have to say no to being treated like second-class citizens. By continuing to say no to a misguided understanding of women's roles, women then can fully and courageously say yes!

So let us hear from these women whose stories are often ignored and who often go unnamed. Our culture often says no, and some of the positions in the church that women may feel called to serve say no. And perhaps women's own sense of inferiority or shame or lack of faith in themselves says no. Nonetheless, God says yes. And if God says yes, then women's response can be an overwhelming *yes* to God. Women can be the bearers of the message that we are all sacred in the eyes of God. Male and female alike, no one should be treated as invisible or left out. We are all precious in God's sight.

B. Story and Questions to Ponder

Brenda attended a business conference. It was her first conference after having accepted employment in a new company. She was sitting at a round table with six male employees who seemed familiar with each other and were involved in a very lively discussion. No one spoke to Brenda or even said hello. She already felt uncomfortable since she was the only female in a leadership role in this company and therefore, the only female at this conference. She made several attempts to enter into conversation, but those at the table continued to speak around her. No one introduced themselves to her or asked her name. She attempted desperately to be included in the group, and she felt like screaming, "See me? I'm *here!*" After several failed attempts at being noticed, she sat silently and wondered if something was hanging out that shouldn't be. She ran to the bathroom to quickly look in the mirror to see if something was dangling from her tooth or coming out of an ear. But no—she looked okay. Before sitting down again, she approached the bar for a refill of her drink, when one of the men from her table came toward her, looking as if he was going to speak. She felt a sense of relief. However, as he approached her, he took hold of the sleeve of her pinstriped suit. He held on to it for a few seconds, then looked her in the eye and said, "You know, the closer the stripe, the more expensive the suit." He then walked away. Brenda just stood there, amazed and stunned that those were the only words spoken to her. *He didn't see me*, she thought. *But what did he see?*

1. What is the message given with the words, "The closer the stripe, the more expensive the suit"?

2. If you were Brenda, how would you respond?

3. Have you ever been in a situation where someone treated you as if you were invisible, or did not count? Have you ever treated someone as if he or she was invisible? Can you describe the situation and what happened?

4. If everyone truly believed that we are all made in the image of God, how would that change the way we treat each other?

CHAPTER 2

The Many Faces of God—What Does God Look Like?

A. Famous Artwork

1. Creation of Adam

If you were asked to draw a picture of God, what would you draw? Perhaps some early artwork will give us an idea of how early artists depicted God. One that is exceptionally powerful and famous is the artwork on the ceiling of the Sistine Chapel. It is called the *Creation of Adam*. This piece of artwork illustrates the creation story from the book of Genesis in which God the Father breathes life into Adam, the first man. This was painted by Michelangelo in 1511. The image of God in this piece of art is of a bearded old man, wrapped in a cloak that he shares with an angel. His left arm is wrapped around a female figure, who has been interpreted by some as Eve, who is not yet created. God's right arm is outstretched to give the spark of life from his finger into that of Adam, whose left arm is extended in a pose that is similar to God's pose. God's finger and Adam's finger are separated by a slight distance.[2]

2. Elohim Creating Adam

Another famous work of art is *Elohim Creating Adam*. Elohim is a Hebrew name for God, and this artwork was created by William Blake in 1795. This piece of art illustrates the passage in the book of Genesis that reads, "And the Lord God formed man of the dust of the ground" (Genesis 2:7). Adam in this painting is shown growing out of the earth, a piece of which Elohim holds in his left hand. This artist believed that the fall of man took place not in the garden of Eden but at the time of creation shown in this art piece, where man is dragged from the material world into the spiritual world. Again in this picture, we have a similar image of God as is seen on the ceiling of the Sistine Chapel—that of a father figure, an older bearded man, creating.

B. Children's Images of God

Here we have an interesting study regarding children's images of God. There was a study done by Helmut Hanisch entitled, "Children and young people's drawings of God." He introduced his study at the University in Germany in 2002.[3] He wanted to know how children visualized God. When he studied their drawings, he found four main themes in their art. They depicted God in four different ways:

- God as a man
- God as a ghost
- God as a face
- God as a woman

Most of the children chose to draw God as a man. The professor who did this study concluded that most children chose to draw God as a man because religion is mediated through father images. In this context, he stated that we have to remember that Sigmund Freud called God the "Super-Father." Altogether, 75 percent of the children in his study depicted God as a man.[4]

Sixteen percent chose to depict God as a ghost. One explanation for depicting God as a ghost is that the children knew that God was invisible, so they knew they could not draw God as a real human being. Some then drew God as a human being with dotted lines, or they drew a cloud with a face or an eerie, ghostlike being.[5]

Six percent of the children drew God simply with a face. The explanation for this is that they knew God could not be depicted as a human being, yet they didn't have any idea how else to draw God. Many who drew faces put the word *God* next to their drawing. They wanted to make sure that the person who looked at their picture knew that the face was meant to be God.

Only 3 percent of the children drew God as a woman. Interestingly enough, it was seven-year-old girls who used this image. David Heller, who is an American Christian educator, said that there was a psychological explanation for this. He said that we could assume that the seven-year-old girls projected themselves into their drawings. Maybe they wanted to emphasize that God loved them or that they received God's attention.

In this study, there were certain characteristics attributed to God. First, God was depicted with a beard, which symbolized old age. The children knew God must be old because he existed before the world was created. Another characteristic was that God lived in the clouds. For most of the children, somewhere in the clouds was where heaven was located. A third symbol or characteristic of God was that God was depicted with wings and halos. The children knew the angels had wings, and God lived with the angels, and therefore God had wings or halos as well.

C. Comparison

If the children's drawings are compared with the famous artwork depicting God, one is able to see that in some ways, they coincide. Artists and children see God as a white male, sometimes with a long, white, flowing beard and a long, white, flowing gown—usually up above someplace looking down below. God is being a Father, a Creator.

These images of God depicted in art, and the images of God from the eyes of these children, certainly reveal how much culture influences one's image of God. This image of God coincides with the worldview that traces back to the Greeks. During the time of Jesus, the prevailing tradition of the Roman world and the Greek world saw society as layered in higher and lower forms of human beings. Roman law, at the time of Jesus, attributed to women a very low status; the wife was the property of her husband. He could punish her in any way he liked. And as far as family property was concerned, the wife did not own anything. Everything she or her children inherited belonged to her husband, including the dowry she brought with her to her marriage. In Roman civil law, women's rights were also very limited. The reason given in Roman law for restraining women's rights is variously described as "the weakness of her sex." This context makes clear that the problem did not lie in women's physical weakness but in what was perceived as her lack of sound judgment and her inability to think logically.[6]

This is what Tertullian said,

> Do you not realize that you are each an Eve? The curse of God on this sex of yours lives on even in our times. Guilty, you must bear its hardships. You are the gateway of the devil; you desecrated the fatal tree; you were the first to betray the law of God, you softened up with your cajoling words the one against whom the devil could not prevail

by force. All too easily you destroyed the image of God, Adam. You are the one who deserved death; because of you the son of God had to die.[7]

There are also dozens of such statements that one finds in the writings of Augustine. He said this:

> Woman does not possess the image of God in herself, but only when taken together with the male who is her head, so that the whole substance is one image. But when she is assigned the role as helpmate, a function that pertains to her alone, then she is not the image of God. But as far as the man is concerned, he is by himself alone the image of God just as fully and completely as when he and the woman are joined together into one.[8]

It is not surprising, then, that this understanding of women as a lower class greatly influenced the judgment of the early fathers of the church. The inferior status of women was simply accepted by the early church fathers—from Irenaeus to Tertullian to Jerome to Ambrosiastor. One finds in the Decretum Gratiani (AD 1140), on which church law was based until 1917, that Ambrosiastor ascribed a woman's state of subjection to her role in sin. He stated,

> Women must cover their heads because they are not the image of God. They must do this as a sign of their subjection to authority and because sin came into the world through them. Their heads must be covered in church in order to honor the bishop. In like manner they have no authority to speak because the bishop is the embodiment of Christ. They must thus act before the bishop as before Christ, the judge, since the bishop is the representative of

the Lord. Because of original sin they must show themselves submissive.[9]

Even written in one of the documents from the Church Council of Constantinople of 692 reads,

> Women are not permitted to speak at the time of the Divine Liturgy. Let them be silent. For it is not permitted for them to speak, but to be in subjection, as the law also said—but if they wish to learn anything let them ask their husbands at home.[10]

One theologian even wrote a lecture that he called: "Eighteen reasons why women are worse off than men." He was giving a lecture on why women could not be ordained. This is his reasoning:

> Women are unfit to receive ordination, for ordination is reserved for perfect members of the church, and, since women are not perfect members of the church, only men are, women are not the image of God, only man is.[11]

The church has made many attempts to rectify the past church traditions by stating in some church documents that women and men are equal and even complement each other. However, sometimes their attempts backfire. For example, one reads in the present Catholic Catechism 370 this phrase: "God is neither male nor female. He is spirit."[12] What a contradiction! Nothing like making a significant point in the first sentence (God is neither male nor female) and messing it up in the second (He is spirit). It's like taking one step forward and two steps back! If God is a spirit, then God is not a He.

In conclusion, the Greek and Roman worldview was patriarchal, and this patriarchal worldview greatly influenced how one imaged

God and what face was given to God—unfortunately, to the detriment of other images of God that have been ignored or forgotten.

D. Patriarchal Worldview

Webster defines patriarchy as composed of two elements. Patriarchy is first, a system of society or government in which the father or eldest male is head of the family and descent is traced through the male line. The second element is that men hold the power and women are largely excluded from it.[13] Good examples of this would be the feudal lord, the abbot in his monastery, the divine right monarch, the priest in his parish, the white European in his colonies, and the husband in relation to his wife. These are all father figures caring for the "children" over whom God has placed them. The difference, of course, between these extensions of patriarchy and its original locus, the family, is that these "children" are adults, and unlike real children, they are expected never to grow up. Thus, in a patriarchal system, most people will remain subordinate all their lives. They cannot protest against this arrangement without challenging God "himself," who is the first patriarch and the legitimator of all others.[14]

While not all men are patriarchs, women rarely are. Where patriarchy reigns, women are subject to men. The man may be father, husband, slaveholder, or priest, but the woman is always a minor.

According to Plato and Aristotle, women are inferior by nature. According to Plato, women came about through a physical degeneration of the human being. He is quoted as saying,

> It is only males who are created directly by the gods and are given souls. Those who live rightly return to the stars, but those who are "cowards" or lead unrighteous lives may with reason be supposed to have changed into the nature of women in the second generation.[15]

Aristotle also considered women to be "defective" males. In his writings, he states that the reason why man dominates in society is his superior intelligence. Only the man is a full human being. "The relationship between the male and the female is by nature such that the male is higher, the female lower, that the male rules and the female is ruled."[16]

One of the most significant writers in Catholic tradition who most influenced the patriarchal way of thinking is Thomas Aquinas. Aquinas accepted, as part of the Aristotelian heritage, which he was shaping into Christian language, was the notion of ancient Greek biology, which believed that the male seed carried all the potency for new life. He furthermore figured that under optimum conditions, men, who are the pinnacle of creation, would reproduce their own perfection and create sons. The fact is, however, that they do not at least half of the time. Instead they generate daughters, who fall short of the perfection of the male seed. This indicates that the man was not "up to par" at the time of intercourse. Perhaps "his seed was damaged" or he was "short on energy due to hot, humid weather."[17]

As regards the individual, Aquinas's conclusion is that the female is something of a "defective male." He believed that the seed of the male tends to produce something like itself, perfect in masculinity. But the procreation of a female is the result either of some change effected by "external influences, like the south wind, for example, which is damp."[18]

Aquinas reaches another conclusion, which is that women's defective state also means their souls are likewise defective. Women's minds are weak and their will is fragile. For their own good they need to be governed by others wiser than themselves. From women's natural inferiority in the order of creation, Aquinas deduces a host of consequences, such as that children should love their fathers more than their mothers since the father is more eminent. Women may not be ordained priests since priesthood signifies the eminence of Christ, and women do not signify what pertains to eminence.

Women also should not preach, since this is an exercise of wisdom and authority of which they are not capable.[19]

Many religious denominations have been affected by this kind of patriarchy, not just the Catholic Church. But as we concentrate on the history of the Catholic Church, prior to the last thirty or so years, the leadership function, as well as the teaching, preaching, and presiding roles, along with the decision-making power, has been limited to the male clergy. Since the Second Vatican Council, there have been many attempts at change, and it is still an ongoing challenge.

That the church developed a patriarchal structure is not surprising because the church emerged in a society that was deeply rooted in patriarchy. What is surprising, however, is that in parts of the Christian scriptures and the earliest Christian communities, we find a sense of egalitarianism that is new to the world around it. The stories of the birth of Jesus gave evidence of the inclusivity of the early Christian by describing the appearance of the angels to the shepherds, who were considered the low and unclean members of the Jewish society, and the coming of foreign magicians bringing gifts to the newborn. Jesus himself attacked the Jewish holiness code that was firmly founded on a male ruling class. Jesus opened himself to all the outcasts and marginalized people, eating with tax collectors and sinners. Some of his close followers were women, who were the first witnesses to the resurrection. In the early Christian communities, women were leaders of small communities, which were called house churches. And even Paul, who could be at times very exclusive, had an image of a community in which there would be no ethnic, social, or gender distinction because all are one in Christ Jesus (Galatians 3:24).

Elizabeth Johnson summarized it well when she states,

> In the light of the original gospel story ... it becomes
> clear that the heart of the problem is not that Jesus
> was a man but that more men are not like Jesus,

insofar as patriarchy defines their self-identity and relationships. Reading Scripture through feminist hermeneutics makes it possible to affirm that despite subsequent distortion something more than the subordination of women is possible, for Jesus.[20]

E. Patriarchy versus Paternity

Before concluding this section, it is important to distinguish sharply between patriarchy on the one hand and fatherhood on the other. The association of fatherhood with patriarchy is so long-standing and widespread that the equation of the two is quite understandable and very often perfectly accurate. However, it is possible for a man to be a father to his children without assuming absolute power over them and to remain a father in relation to adult children whose autonomy and equality with himself he fully accepts. Likewise, it is possible for God to be experienced as paternal without being experienced as a patriarch. And a Father-God who is not experienced as a patriarch can equally well be experienced as a Mother-God without loss of status.

Because we have been so influenced by patriarchy, it has had a great influence on how we image God. There are other images of God that need to be named and reclaimed. Certainly God may be like a Father-Creator, but it is important not to limit God solely to that image, because God is so much more. God is not only Father-Creator. God is not just a God who is up there somewhere or separated from human beings. God is also within creation, a God who is neither male nor female but has both masculine and feminine characteristics at the same time. Let's make a resounding *yes* to this God who is beyond our imagining!

F. Story and Questions to Ponder

Recently, in an elementary parochial school, a teacher asked her third-grade students to use up the remaining time before lunch to take their crayons and draw something creative. While going up and down the rows of students checking their work, she stopped and asked a little girl what she was drawing. She answered, "I'm drawing a picture of God." Her teacher responded that that is impossible since no one knows what God looks like. Her response was, "Well, when I finish they'll know."[21]

1. What image of God from the Old Testament and New Testament best expresses for you the face of God?

2. What was the image of God from your childhood? If you had been asked as a child to draw a picture of God, what would you have drawn?

3. What best expresses for you the face of God today? How did you arrive at this image? (Someone special, life experience, prayer, retreat experiences, spiritual direction, etc.)

CHAPTER 3

Old Testament Names and Images of God

The Old Testament introduces not only male names and images of God but female names and images as well as nongender and nonhuman images of God.

Let's begin by exploring the ones that are most familiar, and that is the male names and images of God.

A. Male Names and Images of God

1. Yahweh

This is the most recognized name for God in the Old Testament. It is found over sixty-seven hundred times throughout the Old Testament. Those of the Jewish faith do not even pronounce this name since it is considered too holy to even verbalize. The Bible story of Moses in Exodus 3:13–14 is the best-known story where God reveals God's name, Yahweh:

> "But," said Moses to God, "if I go to the Israelites and say to them, 'The God of your Ancestors has sent me to you,' and they ask me, 'What is his name?' what do I tell them? God replied to Moses: I am who I am. Then he added: This is what you

will tell them. I AM has sent me to you." (Exodus 3:13–14)

2. Elohim

We see the word Elohim in the very first verse of scripture, Genesis 1:1: "In the beginning God [Elohim] created the heavens and the earth." The Hebrew word for God, Elohim is the plural form of Eloah and it is used in the Old Testament more than any other word for God. The plural ending "-im" has caused many to conclude that God is a plurality of persons, or even multiple deities. It is a unique title for God. It occurs only in Hebrew and in no other ancient Semitic language.

3. Adonai

This word itself can be translated as Lord or Master. It is found 434 times in the Old Testament. It occurs two hundred times in Ezekiel alone and appears eleven times in the book of Daniel.[22] Adonai means *Lord* and was often used as a substitute for God's name "Yahweh" or "Jehovah" (these are interchangeable) in the Old Testament.

The Hebrews felt that God's name was too sacred to pronounce, so they eliminated the vowels and used YHWH, which was unpronounceable. Still, they had to be clear about whom they meant so they often spoke of Adonai, the *Lord* who is *God*. If this name was used to mean someone other than God, "Adonai" was used, which was a common word for one who was a master and ruler.

Psalm 110:1 provides a good starting point to understand who "Adonai" is: "The Lord [YHWH] said to my Lord [Adonai], 'Sit at My right hand, till I make your enemies your footstool.'"

4. Spouse

Spouse is found in the books of Hosea 1–3, Jeremiah 2, and Song of Songs. One of the most beautiful readings in scripture with the theme of God as spouse is found in the Canticle of Canticles, or also called the Song of Songs or the Canticle of Songs.

Christians admitted the canonicity of the Songs of Songs from the beginning, but after Jewish exegetes began to read the Song of Songs allegorically, as having to do with God's love for his people, Christian exegetes followed suit, treating the love that it celebrates as an analogy for the love between God and the church.

> "It will come about in that day," declares the LORD, "That you will call Me Ishi and will no longer call Me Baali. For I will remove the names of the Baals from her mouth so that they will be mentioned by their names no more. In that day I will also make a covenant for them with the beasts of the field, the birds of the sky and the creeping things of the ground. And I will abolish the bow, the sword and war from the land, and will make them lie down in safety. I will betroth you to Me forever; Yes, I will betroth you to Me in righteousness and in justice, In lovingkindness and in compassion, And I will betroth you to Me in faithfulness. Then you will know the LORD. (Hosea 2:16–20)

5. Father

This title is pervasive throughout the Old as well as the New Testament.

Just as God as Spouse is reflected in the Old Testament as God's relationship with Israel, so too is the image of God as Father. One of the most beautiful passages reflecting this relationship is from Isaiah:

But now, O Lord, You are our Father, We are the
clay, and you our potter, and all of us are the work
of Your Hand. (Isaiah 64:8)

The Father-Son motif is a reflection of Israel's relationship with
God. Deeply embedded within their history, Israel's identification
with their God is pictured through a familial relationship. It was
God who promised to deliver his children out of the land of Egypt.
Because Pharaoh refused to liberate the children of Israel, the tenth
plague was the final warning to Pharaoh. Israel is God's firstborn
son chosen from all other nations. Not because of their size (they
were small in number), but God graciously chose the people of Israel
because of His compassion and mercy.

6. Ruler

The most well-known example of the word *ruler* used as a name
of Jesus (*Yeshua'*) is in Micah's prophecy about Jesus the Supreme
Ruler, Christ. The prophecy also says that this Ruler would be a
shepherd. King David was a shepherd before he became the king of
Israel. People expected the Messiah to come as a shepherd-ruler, as
a greater David.

But as for you, Bethlehem Ephrathah, too little to be among
the clans of Judah, from you One will go forth for me to be ruler in
Israel. His goings forth are from long ago, from the days of eternity.
(Micah 5:2)

7. King

When God revealed himself to the patriarchs, it was as God
Almighty or God Most High. To Moses it was Yahweh, I AM. But
when a nation was brought out of Egypt, God is revealed as their
King. The Song of Moses concludes with the triumphant words:
"The LORD will reign for ever and ever" (Exodus 15:18).

8. Shepherd

The following passage from the book of Ezekiel is one that is the most outstanding in its imagery of sheep and shepherd:

> For thus says the Lord God, "Behold, I Myself will search for my sheep and seek them out. As a shepherd cares for his herd in the day when he is among his scattered sheep, so I will care for my sheep and will deliver them from all the places to which they were scattered on a cloudy and gloomy day". (Ezekiel 34:11–12)

Psalm 23 is most likely one of the most beloved of all the psalms and perhaps even one of the most beloved passages of all of scripture. Sheep are basically helpless creatures who cannot survive long without a shepherd, upon whose care they are totally dependent.[23] Sheep are animals that can't see very well, nor do they hear very well. They are slow and therefore find it difficult to escape predators. They have no camouflage, no weapons, such as claws, sharp hooves, or powerful jaws for self-defense. Sheep are easily confused and frightened. How much are we like sheep, going astray, getting lost? Protection for the sheep is the shepherd—God is like a shepherd to us. If we get lost, lose our way, it is the shepherd who looks after us, who searches for the lost, and who shows us the way to safety. God is our Good shepherd.

> The Lord is my shepherd; there is nothing I lack. In green pastures he makes me lie down; to still waters he leads me; he restores my soul. He guides me along right paths for the sake of his name. Even though I walk through the valley of the shadow of death, I will fear no evil, for you are with me; your rod and your staff comfort me. (Psalm 23)

I will appoint for you shepherds after my own
heart, who will shepherd you wisely and prudently.
(Jeremiah 3:15)

9. Vineyard Owner

The Song of the Vineyard is found in Isaiah 5:1–7.

> For the vineyard of the LORD of hosts is the house
> of Israel and the men of Judah His delightful plant.
> Thus He looked for justice, but behold, bloodshed;
> for righteousness, but behold, a cry of distress.

Summary

In the Old Testament, the concept of Yahweh represents a Supreme
Being who is absolute, eternal, unchanging. Not only is this Supreme
Being the Creator of the Universe, but this Being is a personal being
who cares intensely for humankind as a father does for his child or
a husband does for his wife. This Supreme Being is described as
merciful, wise, righteous, kind, just, compassionate, and patient.
However, this Loving Being is also described as jealous. There are
many passages in the Old Testament that display this jealous God,
who will harshly punish. A good example of the jealous God can be
found in Exodus 34, where God appears to Moses just after Moses
ascends Mt. Sinai to receive the Ten Commandments a second time:

> So the LORD passed before him and proclaimed:
> The LORD, the LORD, a God gracious and merciful,
> slow to anger and abounding in love and fidelity,
> continuing his love for a thousand generations,
> and forgiving wickedness, rebellion, and sin; yet
> not declaring the guilty guiltless, but bringing
> punishment for their parents' wickedness on

children and children's children to the third and
fourth generation! (Exodus 34:6–7)

B. Female Names and Images of God

The Old Testament is filled with female images of God. Many
of those images are maternal (conceiving, carrying in her womb,
experiencing labor pains, giving birth, nursing, feeding, washing,
teaching, comforting, protecting).

1. Mother

Of all of the prophets, Isaiah appears the most comfortable in
describing God as a Mother-God. The womb was our first home,
and all of us were born from our mothers. "What better image can
there be for expressing the most basic reality of existence: that we
live and move and have our being in God?"[24] This is obvious in these
four passages:

> I (God) have kept silent for a long time, I have kept
> still and restrained myself. Now like a woman in labor
> I will groan, I will both gasp and pant. (Isaiah 42:14)

> As a mother comforts her child, so I will comfort
> you; and you will be comforted in Jerusalem. (Isaiah
> 66:13)

> Can a mother forget the baby at her breast and have
> no compassion on the child she has borne? Though
> she may forget, I [God] will not forget you! (Isaiah
> 49:15)

> For thus says the LORD, "Behold, I extend peace to
> her like a river, and the glory of the nations like an

overflowing stream; and you will be nursed, you
will be carried on the hip and fondled on the knees.
(Isaiah 66:12)

Using female metaphors for God is not a radical feminist
innovation. It was part of early Christian history. Medieval mystic
Meister Eckhart described God's activity: "What does God do all
day long? God gives birth. From all eternity God lies on a maternity
bed giving birth."[25]

There are some passages, especially in the Old Testament that
can be attributed to Mother-God or Father-God—for example, in
this passage from Hosea:

> When Israel was a child, I loved him, and out of
> Egypt I called my son. The more I called them, the
> more they went from me; they kept sacrificing to
> the Baals, and offering incense to idols. Yet it was I
> who taught Ephraim to walk, I took them up in my
> arms; but they did not know that I healed them. I
> led them with cords of human kindness, with bands
> of love. I was to them like those who lift infants to
> their cheeks. I bent down to them and fed them.
> (Hosea 11:1–4)

The picture in one's mind, or the mind of the author here, might
be of a mother or a father, but no words are used that betray the
gender of the parent. There are other passages in the Old Testament
that describe God as Maternal: Isaiah 49:14, 66:12, Hosea 11:1–4,
Numbers 11:10–14, Wisdom 16:20, Ruth 1:16, Job 38:28–29.

2. Lady Wisdom

This theme of God as Lady Wisdom is found throughout the book
of Wisdom as well as Proverbs.

> Wisdom cries aloud in the street, in the open squares she raises her voice; Down the crowded ways she calls out, at the city gates she utters her words. (Proverbs 20:21–22)

C. Nongender Names and Images of God

1. Creator

This image of God as Creator is found in twenty-seven books of the Bible, but is most common in the book of Genesis. Genesis 1:1 says, "In the beginning God created the heaven and the earth."

Genesis 1:7 says, "And God made the firmament, and divided the waters which were under the firmament from the waters which were above the firmament: and it was so."

2. Helper

These passages remind us, that, even though we might live in uncertain times, God is not uncertain. God will always be there to help. God will never abandon God's people.

> For he said, "The God of my father is my help, and has rescued me from Pharaoh's sword." (Exodus 18:4)

> The house of Israel trusts in the LORD, who is their help and shield. The house of Aaron trusts in the LORD, who is their help and shield. Those who fear the LORD trust in the LORD, who is their help and shield. (Psalm 115:9–11)

> Our help is in the name of the LORD, the maker of heaven and earth. (Psalm 124:8)

3. Savior

The word *Savior* is used throughout the Old Testament, especially in Exodus and the Prophets. But one of the most beautiful passages that indicate the saving power of God is found in Mary's prayer, the Magnificat, when she states, "My soul exalts the Lord, and my spirit has rejoiced in God my Savior" (Luke 1:46).

4. Potter

In the days of Jeremiah, all pottery was for some specific use. The clay was shaped and formed into vessels, and all vessels were not alike. A potter is patient. The potter shapes and reshapes the vessels until it is uniquely and wonderfully made.

> Can I not do to you, house of Israel, as this potter has done? Indeed, like clay in the hand of the potter, so are you in my hand, house of Israel. (Jeremiah 18:6)

D. Nonhuman Names and Images of God

1. Eagle

There are actually thirty-three Bible verses referring to eagles. The eagle, with its keen eyes, symbolized courage, strength, and immortality, and is also considered the "king of the skies." The eagle became a symbol of power and strength in Ancient Rome.

> As an eagle incites its nestlings, hovering over its young. So he spread wings, took them, bore them upon his pinions. (Deuteronomy 32:11)

2. Lion

There are thirty-seven Bible verses that refer to lions and ten passages that refer to God as a lion.

> For I am like a lion to Ephraim, like a young lion to the house of Judah; it is I who tear the prey and depart, I carry it away and no one can save it. (Hosea 5:14)

> They will walk after the LORD. He will roar like a lion; Indeed He will roar. And His sons will come trembling from the west. (Hosea 11:10)

> He has left His hiding place like the lion; for their land has become a horror because of the fierceness of the oppressing sword and because of His fierce anger. (Jeremiah 25:38)

3. Rock

The word *rock* is equated with the idea of strength. Rock was used to build walls, fortresses, and towers in biblical times. God is our source of strength in times of distress and danger.

> So Jacob ate and was satisfied, Jeshurun grew fat and you became fat and gross and gorged. They forsook the God who made them and scorned the Rock of their salvation. (Deuteronomy 32:15)

> Trust in the LORD forever! For the LORD is an eternal Rock. (Isaiah 26:4)

4. Wind

One can think of God as like the wind. It is invisible, mysterious, and powerful. You cannot control the wind, and you can't have life without wind. Wind gives life. Such is God—invisible, mysterious, powerful—a God you can't control, who gives life to the whole world.

> Then the LORD said: Go out and stand on the mountain before the LORD; the LORD will pass by. There was a strong and violent wind rending the mountains and crushing rocks before the LORD— but The LORD was not in the wind; after the wind, an earthquake—but the LORD was not in the earthquake; after the earthquake, fire—but the LORD was not in the fire; after the fire, a light silent sound. (1 Kings 19:11–13)

5. Fire

In this physical world, fire can be our friend or our foe. It can bring us comfort as well as tragedy. It is the same in the spiritual world. This startling description of God as a "consuming fire" is found in both the Old and New Testaments. When Moses exhorted the children of Israel to be obedient to the word of God, this passage from Deuteronomy is the message that Moses gave to the children of Israel.

> For the LORD, your God, is a consuming fire, a jealous God. (Deuteronomy 4:24)

6. Fountain, Spring of Water

God is the source of living water. God spreads God's reign. If one also reads Psalm 72:6 and Psalm 46:4 one can see that our God is a flowing God, and this God spreads God's reign and kingdom over the whole earth by flowing as a river and water of life.

Two evils my people have done: they have forsaken me, the source of living water. They have dug themselves cisterns, broken cisterns that cannot hold water. (Jeremiah 2:13)

E. Conclusion

If one spends some time reading these passages in the Old Testament, one will soon discover that God is much more than any one image or name. Limiting the understanding of God into just one or two images or names puts a limitation on God. Regina Coll, in her book *Christianity and Feminism in Conversation,* puts it so well when she states,

> Metaphors tell us something about God, but, at the same time hides something about God. What Father reveals, King does not, what Mother reveals, Shepherd does not. Metaphors are not definitions or even descriptions; they always limp a little. Because metaphors both reveal and conceal, it is a kind of idolatry to use only one metaphor for God. To do so is to imply that we have captured who God is. We have boxed God in, so to speak. We have named God. The first reason to multiply our metaphors for God is to acknowledge that God is beyond anything we may say.[26]

This says something to us about using only male names and images of God. When, for example, God is described as "Father," that says something wonderful about fathers, and it certainly is not inappropriate to use the name Father in describing God. The problem comes about when only the word *Father* is used to describe God. When that happens, that implies that we know all about God, and there is nothing more to learn. What if we add our understanding of God to include such images as Helper, Comforter, Rock, Fountain, and Spring of Water? What if we add the Mother image to God? What does that add to our understanding of who God is or what God is like? For a child, mothering is associated with a human experience of comfort, security, nurture, compassion—a beautiful and fuller image of what God is like. Pope John Paul I startled the world in 1978 with his reference to divine maternity.

> God is our Father, even more God is our mother. God does not want to hurt us, but only to do good for us, all of us. If children are ill, they have additional claim to be loved by their mother. And, we, too, if by chance we are sick with badness and are on the wrong track, have yet another claim to be loved by the Lord. [27]

But again, by using the Mother Image for God does not mean that we exclude the Father image for God. God is mystery, and a mystery cannot be confined to any one set of names or images, but transcends them all.[28]

F. Story and Questions to Ponder

Long before I became familiar with the academic debates concerning calling God "Mother," debates that I am now currently a part of as a professor at Princeton Theological Seminary, I was being raised in a household where I instinctively understood that the divine presence was manifest in the loving hands and arms of mothers, and most especially in the life of my grandmother who raised me. My grandmother's kitchen was a theological laboratory where she taught me how to love people just as naturally as she taught me to make peach cobbler and buttermilk biscuits. I watched and listened as she ministered to the sick and the lost, with a Bible in one hand and a freshly baked pound cake in the other, despite having no official ministry role. I knew that if God was real, if God truly loved me as a parent loves a child, then God was also "Mother" and not only "Father." Only years of dogma and doctrine force you to unlearn what you know to be true in your own heart, demanding "Father" as the only acceptable appellation and concept for God.[29]

1. Of the Old Testament images of God, what best describes for you who God is?

2. What is the one image of God that you are least attracted to?

3. Can you write your own prayer, addressing God with the description or image that you can relate to the most?

CHAPTER 4

New Testament Names and Images of God

Jesus revolutionizes our understanding of God and offers a new approach to understanding who God is. He also introduces us to male as well as female images of God, and also offers us male as well as female descriptions of the kingdom of God.

A. Male, Female, Nongender, and Nonhuman Images of God

1. I am

> God is spirit, and those who worship Him must worship in Spirit and truth. The woman said to Him, "I know that Messiah is coming (He who is called Christ); when that One comes, he will declare all things to us. Jesus said to her, "I who speak to you am He." (John 4:24–26)

> Your father Abraham rejoiced to see my day, and he saw it and was glad. So the Jews said to Him, "You are not yet fifty years old, and have you seen Abraham?" Jesus said to them, "Truly, truly, I say to you, before Abraham was born, I am." (John 8:56–58)

2. Father or Abba

The Aramaic term *Abba* appears three times in the Greek New Testament of The Bible. Each time the term appears, it is followed immediately by the translation *ho pater* in Greek, which literally means "the father." In each case, it is used with reference to God. Mark records that Jesus used the term when praying in Gethsemane shortly before his death, saying: "*Abba*, Father, all things are possible to you; remove this cup from me. Yet not what I want, but what you want" (Mark 14:36). The two other occurrences are in Paul's letters, in Romans 8:15 and Galatians 4:6. It seems evident from these texts that, in apostolic times, the Christians made use of the term *Abba* in their prayers to God.

> For even if there are so-called gods whether in heaven or on earth, as indeed there are Gods and many lords, yet for us there is but one God, the Father, from whom are all things and we exist for Him; and one Lord, Jesus Christ, by whom are all things, and we exist through Him. (2 Corinthians 8:4–6)

3. King

The idea of Jesus being King of Kings and Lord of Lords means that there is no higher authority. His reign over all things is absolute. Jesus was raised from the dead and placed over all things.

> Far above all rule and authority and power and dominion, and above every name that is named not only in this age but also in the one to come. (Ephesians 1:21)

Now to the King eternal, immortal, invisible, the only God, be honor and glory forever and ever Amen. (1 Timothy 1:17)

Sing praise to God, sing praise: sing praise to our King, sing praise. (Psalm 47:7)

4. Mother Hen

In the following passage from Luke's gospel, Jesus reveals God's searching, aching love as a mother hen who would gather all her chicks under her safe, protective wings. At the same time, the mother hen can be quite fierce in guarding her young from the predators that stalk them. She will give her life to stand between danger and her chicks. The love shown by a mother hen is the kind of gathering, protective love that God reveals. It is one that reaches out and warns against dangers. It is one that keeps the chicks close for their safety and welfare.

O Jerusalem, Jerusalem, the city that kills the prophets and stones those sent to her! How often I wanted to gather your children together, just as a hen gathers her brood under her wings, and you would not have it. (Luke 13:34)

5. Love

The original Greek used to write the New Testament shows that there is more than one word for love. The Greek word *agapos*, often referred to as agape love, is the word used in 1 John 4. It is used when speaking of an unconditional love. This love of God is boundless. God does not only give love but is the source of love. The Creator of all things is the one who created love. It is because of God's love that we are able to love. As 1 John 4:19 states, "We love because he first loved us."

> Beloved, let us love one another, for love is from God; and everyone who loves is born of God and knows God. (1 John 4:7)

6. Light

This is not metaphorical. John does not assert that God is "like light" or that God "can be compared to" light. He states that God is light and contrasts this light to darkness. Darkness is the absence of light. God is light, with no darkness. If we walk in darkness, we cannot truthfully claim that we have union with God.

> This is the message we have heard from Him and announce to you, that God is Light, and in Him there is no darkness at all. (1 John 1:5)

7. Spirit

God is not limited to a physical body. But even though God is spirit, God is also a living, personal being. As such, we can know God personally. Joshua 3:10 speaks of God in this way, saying, "You will know that the living God is among you."

> God is spirit, and those who worship Him must worship in spirit and truth. (John 4:24)

8. Breath/Wind

Wind is symbolic of the Spirit of God, The Hebrew word for Spirit, *Ruach*, is breath, wind, breeze, spirit, air, and strength.

The wind blows where it wishes and you hear the sound of it, but do not know where it comes from and where it is going; so is everyone who is born of the Spirit. (John 3:8)

By the word of the Lord the heavens were made, and by the breath of His mouth all their host. (Psalm 33:6)

9. Fire

The Bible sometimes refers to God as a "consuming fire." This is introduced in Deuteronomy 4:24: "For the Lord your God is a consuming fire, a jealous God." Here the idea of "consuming fire" stands alongside God's jealousy. The context of the chapter deals with God's command not to worship other gods. Only the Lord was to be worshiped. He would not tolerate worship of others. He was a "consuming fire" in the sense that he desired all of the worship of the Israelites.

Therefore, since we receive a kingdom which cannot be shaken, let us show gratitude, and offer to God an acceptable service with reverence and awe, for our God is a consuming fire. (Hebrews 12:28–29)

10. Fountain/Spring of Water

We as Christians and genuine believers in Christ need to do one thing: we need to drink of God as the fountain of living waters! Yes, we need to read the Bible, we need to pray, we need to meet with other saints, and we need to do so many other things, but first and foremost, even as we're doing all the other things, we need to drink God. Our God is a fountain of living waters, and any other water we drink will never satisfy or quench our thirst (John 4:13*)*. How do we drink of God? There are many ways, the simplest of which is calling on the name of the Lord—O Lord Jesus!—from the depth of our being, until living water gushes out![30]

> But whoever drinks of the water that I will give him shall never thirst; but the water I will give him will become in him a well of water springing up to eternal life. (John 4:14)

11. Shepherd Seeking a Lost Sheep

We see here a good example of Jesus's teaching technique. When Jesus gives a male description of God (the shepherd going after the lost sheep), he follows it with a female description of God (the women searching for the lost coin). God is like the shepherd who went after his lost sheep until he found it, just as much as God is like the woman who searched her house until she found her lost coin.

> Now all the tax collectors and the sinners were coming near Him to listen to Him. Both the Pharisees and the scribes began to grumble, saying, "This man receives sinners and eats with them." So He told them this parable, saying, "What man among you, if he has a hundred sheep and has lost one of them, does not leave the ninety-nine in the open pasture and go after the one which is lost until he finds it? When he has found it, he lays it on his shoulders, rejoicing. And when he comes home, he calls together his friends and his neighbors, saying to them, 'Rejoice with me, for I have found my sheep which was lost!' I tell you that in the same way, there will be more joy in heaven over one

sinner who repents than over ninety-nine righteous persons who need no repentance. (Luke 15:1–6)

12. The Woman Seeking the Lost Coin

Or what woman having ten coins and losing one would not light a lamp and sweep the house, searching carefully until she finds it? And when she does find it, she calls together her friends and neighbors and says to them, "Rejoice with me because I have found the coin that I lost. In just the same way, I tell you, there will be rejoicing among the angels of God over one sinner who repents" (Luke 15:8–10)

It is the same with the story of the kingdom being like the mustard seed in Matthew 13:31.

He proposed another parable to them. "The kingdom of heaven is like a mustard seed that a person took and sowed in a field. It is the smallest of all the seeds, yet when full-grown it is the largest of all plants. It becomes a large bush, and the birds of the sky come and dwell in its branches."

This parable that is known so well is followed by the parable of the baker woman and how the kingdom is like the yeast that the woman uses when making bread in Matthew 13:33.

He spoke to them another parable. "The kingdom of heaven is like yeast that a woman took and mixed with three measures of wheat flour until the whole batch was leavened."

These are truly inspiring words and images that come to mind when Jesus teaches the crowds about what God is like. Both the good shepherd and the lost coin tell the same story of God's active search for the sinner. In one, a man loses his sheep and leaves his ninety-nine others to seek for it vigorously. When he finds it, he calls upon his neighbors to rejoice. This marvelous image of God has worked its way into the Christian imagination. But the same drama is played out in the next story. A woman loses one of her ten coins and drops everything to search the whole house until she finds it. And when she does, she calls her friends and neighbors to rejoice with her. Here we have another image of God the Redeemer. Jesus is saying that we are as precious to God even when we sin as money is to the woman who lost her coin. God goes after us in the same way. The same message is being proclaimed in both stories—one in terms of male work and one in terms of female work. It is the same with the story Jesus tells of the mustard seed, immediately followed by the story of the baker woman. Both stories reflect the active, consuming love of God. And both symbols are in our tradition. But the imagination of Christians has latched onto one and neglected the other. In a setting reminiscent of Lady Wisdom, Jesus even referred to himself in female imagery, wishing he could gather the people of Jerusalem within his arms as a mother hen gathers chicks under her wings.

> Jerusalem, Jerusalem, who kills the prophets and stones those who are sent to her! How often I wanted to gather your children together, the way a hen gathers her chicks under her wings, and you were unwilling. (Matthew 23:37)

At various times in the Christian tradition, female metaphors for God did come into use. The Syriac liturgy, for example, refers to the Holy Spirit as our mother.[31] The mystic Julian of Norwich understands Jesus as our mother, nourishing us from his own body.[32] And then there was Pope John Paul I, who, as stated earlier, was quoted memorably that just as God is truly our father, even more is God our mother, especially when we are in trouble through sin.[33] In general, however, we have neglected the scriptural and traditional images of God, seldom if ever using them in liturgy, catechesis, or personal prayer. Instead we use the maleness of Jesus to concentrate on a male God.

The history of interpreting what God is like is very much influenced by a patriarchal mind-set. If the mind-set is male and patriarchal, it is hardly possible to be open to an image of God that is not male and patriarchal.

B. God Is Like a Loving Parent

The image that we most closely associate Jesus with, when describing God, is the image of God as Father. Again, it was not that he was emphasizing the fact that God is a male—but that God is like a parent. This was very revolutionary in Jesus's time, and it probably shocked his listeners. He stressed not God as the judging, punishing God, but instead, God more like an intimate, tender parent-God, an Abba or Papa God—a God who is near, like a parent is to a child.

C. The Life of Jesus Reveals the Image of God

Certainly, for the most revolutionary image we have of God we need not look any further than to Jesus himself. If we want to have an image of God and understand who God is, we look to the life of Jesus to understand what Jesus was trying to tell us about God. If we look at Jesus, then we see the face of God. We don't have to go any further than that. Jesus himself is the visible expression of God. But he was also trying to tell us that we don't have to go far to find the face of God, for God's face is in the poor whom you meet. God's face is in the face of those who care for one another, in love, in generosity, in tenderness, in selflessness and self-giving. What

Jesus did was to try to convince people that to love as he loved, one will then discover that the sacred is in our midst. The whole point of Jesus's life is that a human person like us so lived life that other people believed they saw the divine. Jesus called his audience to change their way of thinking. God is here—in your loving, in your caring, in your generosity, and more. God is here—even when you are conscious of your failure, your sin, your low status in life, and when everything seems to be going wrong.

Jesus set the foundation here for what would become a key Christian insight. God is love, and when you live in love, you live in God and God lives in you (1 John 4:16). However, this foundation can stay at the level of a pious thought unless people are led to identify their everyday experiences of goodness and caring with God's presence among them, and do this consistently, faithfully, and confidently.

Jesus saw one of his main tasks in life was not to change an attitude in God, to change God's mind, as it were, but his role was concerned with people changing their mind, the way they perceived the face of God and their relationship with God. Nowhere in his preaching or in his dealings with people is there the slightest hint of the original sin mentality that later became so pervasive in the church's worldview. The gospel evidence of the way Jesus related with children coupled with his teaching about God surely suggests he would have been horrified by the idea of children being born into a state of utter separation from God.

This conclusion, then, from contemplating Jesus's life and preaching is that the divine and the human are intermingled, and that to see a human person living a totally loving, gracious life is to see the face of God. We see the face of God each day in those we meet—and we offer to them our own face. If it is also filled with goodness, care, love, and generosity—they will also be encountering the face of God.

D. Story and Questions to Ponder

John Gillespie Magee Jr. was an American pilot and flew with the Royal Canadian Air Force in World War II. He was killed at the age of nineteen on December 11, 1941, during a training flight. On his grave are inscribed the first and last lines from his poem "High Flight." This section of this poem written by him appears on the headstones of many veterans buried at Arlington National Cemetery, especially aviators and astronauts.

> Up, up the long delirious burning blue
> I've topped the wind-swept heights with easy grace,
> where never lark, or even eagle, flew;
> and, while with silent, lifting mind I've trod
> the high untrespassed sanctity of space,
> put out my hand and touched the face of God.
> —John Gillespie Magee Jr.[34]

1. What does this poem tell us about seeing the face of God?

2. Can you think of any time in your life in which you might have missed the face of God even though God's face, God's wisdom, or God's divine presence was right in front of you?

3. What New Testament image of God are you most attracted to/least attracted to?

4. What face of God would you like others to see in you?

CHAPTER 5

The Neglected Stories of Women
in the Old Testament

A. Historical Perspective

Among Christians of every denomination, Roman Catholics are probably the least knowledgeable concerning the Bible. Roman Catholics were rarely encouraged by church leaders to read the Bible. All of that changed when it came to the Second Vatican Council (1962–1965). But a little historical perspective may be helpful in understanding the status and role of women during the time of the early Israelite community.

The first five books of the Bible are Genesis, Exodus, Leviticus, Numbers, and Deuteronomy. Jewish believers call this the Torah, and Christians refer to it as the Pentateuch, or sometimes referred to as the five books of Moses, since they were originally believed to be written by Moses. Most of the laws of Israel were addressed to men who were responsible to their whole household. The woman's primary responsibility was to respect and obey her husband. She was valuable as the mother of sons. Since daughters left the family home upon marriage, sons could be counted on to carry on the inheritance and the name.

1. Ritual Impurity

It was understood that women in Israel were ritually unclean at the time of their period, after sexual intercourse, and after childbirth. One indication of the attitude about women is that uncleanness lasted seven days after the birth of a son, but fourteen days after the birth of a daughter. This is found in the book of Leviticus:

> Then the LORD spoke to Moses, saying, "Speak to the sons of Israel, saying: When a woman gives birth and bears a male child, then she shall be unclean for seven days, as in the days of her menstruation she shall be unclean. On the eighth day the flesh of his foreskin shall be circumcised. Then she shall remain in the blood of her purification for thirty-three days; she shall not touch any consecrated thing, nor enter the sanctuary until the days of her purification are completed. But if she bears a female child, then she shall be unclean for two weeks, as in her menstruation; and she shall remain in the blood of her purification for sixty-six days." (Leviticus 12:1–5)

Also, in Leviticus 15:19–30, a menstruating woman is considered ritually unclean. "Anyone who touches her will be unclean until evening." Touching her, touching an object she would sit or lay on, or having intercourse with her also makes a person ritually unclean. The extent to which these rules are observed in modern Judaism varies depending on the degree of conservatism or orthodoxy.

Some church fathers defended the exclusion of women from ministry based on a notion of uncleanness, and it is in part responsible for the argument against the ordination of women.[35] Others held that purity laws should be discarded as part of the Old Covenant.

In spite of the restrictions in Leviticus, Jesus allowed himself to be touched by a hemorrhaging woman and cured her (Mark 5:24–25).

2. Divorce

Divorce also was a male privilege. The failure to produce a son was reason enough to get a divorce. In early Israel, the women gave their slaves to their husbands to produce a male who would be counted as the son, not of the slave woman, but of the wife. Or the man simply took another wife. However, in later biblical times divorce seemed to be the more common solution to the problem of the barren wife.[36]

There are many stories and laws found in scripture regarding women that are profoundly troubling.

Women are identified as property (Exodus 20:17, Deuteronomy 5:21, Judges 5:30).

Rape laws require fathers to be paid for damages and the female victim to marry her rapist (Deuteronomy 22:28–29).

Virginity expectations focused almost exclusively on girls, and women are valued less in vow redemption (Leviticus 27:1–8).

The birth of girls represents a greater impurity assessment in the Levitical purity codes (Leviticus 12:2–4).

Women are considered spoils of war (Numbers 31:32–35, Deuteronomy 20:14, 21:10–15, Judges 5:30, 21:11–23), and adultery laws subjected women to more scrutiny and punished them more severely than men. Polygamy was common, owning concubines was common, and impregnating slave women was common.

In summary, and as an introduction to the women in the Old Testament, it is obvious that women had no place in the society at that time. They were defined by patriarchy, and their words and actions were judged only as they affected men's lives. Women in scripture usually have noteworthy roles but are always subordinate to men. Traditionally, women have not been seen as central because of their relationship to a male hero. Mothers, wives, and harlots played important roles in the history of Israel. These same women seen through another lens are recognized as significant in their own lives, contributing to the life and word of Israel, of Jesus, and of the early church. What we want to try to reclaim is the place of women in our own faith history.

B. Deborah

Deborah was a prophet, judge, and charismatic leader of her people—a woman of great strength and courage, whose story nevertheless exalts violence and bloodshed.

Deborah's story is told in the fourth and fifth chapter of the book of Judges. Her name can be translated as "bee." Interestingly enough, science confirms and ancient tradition attests to the fact that of all the animals in the animal kingdom, bees rank among the highest in intelligence. Perhaps we could say as well that Deborah stands out as one of the wisest in the Old Testament. Deborah is the fourth judge of Israel and the only female judge mentioned in the Bible.

When she was judge of Israel, it had been under severe oppression for twenty years. As Judge, she planned a military strategy against the oppressors, appointed a general, and led a victorious battle. Her song of victory is found in Judges 5:1–31 and is considered to be one of the most ancient compositions of the Bible.[37]

> Then Deborah and Barak the son of Abinoam sang on that day, saying, "That the leaders led in Israel, That the people volunteered, Bless the LORD! "Hear, O kings; give ear, O rulers! I—to the LORD, I will sing, I will sing praise to the LORD, the God of Israel. "LORD, when You went out from Seir, When You marched from the field of Edom, The earth quaked, the heavens also dripped, Even the clouds dripped water. "The mountains quaked at

the presence of the LORD, This Sinai, at the presence
of the LORD, the God of Israel. (Judges 5:1–5)

Even though this story is of incredible bravery, it is never read in
the Sunday or daily lectionary readings at Mass. We do hear about
Gideon, Jephthah, and Samson, as well as the two sons of Samuel.
But the only female judge, renowned for her bravery, is never read
at weekday or Sunday liturgies. She is left "standing at the gate."[38]

C. Huldah

The Old Testament introduces its readers to many of the prophets.
But how about Huldah? Her story is found in 2 Chronicles 34:23–
27 as well as 2 Kings 22:14–20.

Huldah was a prophet who lived in Jerusalem during the time
of the prophet Jeremiah. The word Huldah actually means "weasel,"
and that is the same word used to describe one of the tribes in Israel.
Huldah's wisdom and insight were well known to Josiah the king,
and when the wise men came to him with the book of the Law and
they did not know how to interpret it, who did Josiah send them
to? Huldah … He sent his five men who led the nation to Huldah
to interpret the law. It was a woman who set up interpreting the
law for the king of Israel and the five men who led the nation.
Unfortunately, the story of Huldah is excised from the weekday
reading for Wednesday of the twelfth week in ordinary time, year
II. The verses referring to Huldah (15–19) are sliced right out of the
middle of the lectionary passage.[39] (2 Kings 22:8–13; 23:1–3).

So Hilkiah the priest, Ahikam, Achbor, Shaphan,
and Asaiah went to Huldah the prophetess, the wife
of Shallum the son of Tikvah, the son of Harhas,
keeper of the wardrobe, and they spoke to her.
She said to them, "Thus says the LORD God of
Israel, 'Tell the man who sent you to me, thus says

the LORD, "Behold, I bring evil on this place and on its inhabitants, even all the words of the book which the king of Judah has read. Because they have forsaken me and have burned incense to other gods that they might provoke me to anger with all the work of their hands, therefore my wrath burns against this place, and it shall not be quenched." But to the king of Judah who sent you to inquire of the LORD thus shall you say to him, 'Thus says the LORD God of Israel, "Regarding the words which you have heard, because your heart was tender and you humbled yourself before the LORD when you heard what I spoke against this place and against its inhabitants that they should become a desolation and a curse, and you have torn your clothes and wept before me, I truly have heard you," declares the LORD. "Therefore, behold, I will gather you to your fathers, and you will be gathered to your grave in peace, and your eyes will not see all the evil which I will bring on this place. So they brought back word to the king. (2 Kings 22:14–20)

Huldah was certainly a prophet. Could we also dare to say as well that she was called to speak the truth to the powerful in authority—a truth that they did not want to hear? Does that sound like something we are called to do at times? Could Huldah be, for us, a source of strength and encouragement?

D. Esther

There is a book in her honor in the Old Testament. The book of Esther is one of only two books in the Bible named for women. The other is the book of Ruth. Esther was a Jew in the kingdom of Media and Persia. She was raised by her relative Mordecai, after her parents died. Because of her beauty, she was conscripted into the harem of King Ahasuerus, and she eventually became queen. Her cousin Mordecai became a minor official in the Persian government of Susa. Soon after he took that position, he uncovered a plot to assassinate the king. He told Esther about the conspiracy, and she reported to the king Xerxes, giving credit to Mordecai. The plot was thwarted, and Mordecai's act of kindness was preserved. But one of the high officials in the land hated the Jews, and he especially hated Mordecai, who had refused to bow down to him. So Haman devised a scheme to have every Jew in Persia killed. The king bought into the plot and agreed to annihilate the Jewish people on a specific day. Meanwhile, Mordecai learned of the plan and shared it with Esther. Esther then urged all the Jews to fast and pray for deliverance. Then, risking her own life, brave young Esther approached the king with a plan of her own. She invited Xerxes and Haman to a banquet, where eventually she revealed her Jewish heritage to the king, as well as Haman's diabolical plot to have her and her people killed. In a rage, the king ordered Haman to be hung on the gallows—the same gallows that Haman built for Mordecai. Mordecai was promoted to Haman's high position, and Jews were granted protection throughout the land. She used her position to help her people.

Even though she is known for her courage and is considered a great heroine in a time of oppression, there is no account in the lectionary of the bravery with which she saved her people from annihilation. It is never proclaimed in the lectionary. Three other passages from the book of Esther are found in the lectionary (Common of the Saints, #737; and in Masses for Various Occasions #821,876) but not only might these passages never be used in the parishes, all three are accounts of the prayer of Esther's Uncle, Mordecai.

E. Miriam

Miriam is found in four different Old Testament books: Numbers 12:20:1–2, Deuteronomy 24:8–9, 1 Chronicles 6:1–3, and Micah 6:3–4.

Miriam was the sister of Moses and Aaron and shared leadership with them during the exodus from Egypt. She led the women in song and dance after the parting of the Sea of Reeds. She saved Moses's life by convincing Pharaoh's daughter to take him into her household after he was weaned.

Miriam first appears in the book of Exodus not long after Pharaoh decrees that all newborn Hebrew boys will be drowned in the Nile River. Miriam's mother has been hiding Miriam's infant brother, Moses, for three months. But as the child grows older, she decides that it is no longer safe for him at home—after all, it would only take one ill-timed cry for an Egyptian guard to discover the child.

Miriam's mother puts Moses in a waterproof wicker basket and places it in the Nile, hoping the river will carry her son to safety. Miriam follows at a distance and sees the basket float near Pharaoh's daughter, who is bathing in the Nile. Pharaoh's daughter sends one of her servants to fetch the basket from among the reeds and finds Moses when she opens it. She recognizes him as one of the Hebrew babies and feels sympathy for the child.

At this time, Miriam emerges from her hiding place and approaches Pharaoh's daughter, offering to find a Hebrew woman to nurse the child. The princess agrees, and Miriam brings none other than her own mother to care for Moses. "Take this baby and nurse him for me, and I will pay you," Pharaoh's daughter says to her (Exodus 2:9). As a result of Miriam's actions, Moses was raised by his mother until he was weaned, at which time he was adopted by the princes and became a member of the Egyptian royal family.

Miriam does not appear again until much later in the Exodus story. Moses has commanded Pharaoh to let his people go, and God has sent the ten plagues down upon Egypt. The former Hebrew slaves have crossed the Red Sea, and the waters have crashed down upon the Egyptian soldiers who were pursuing them.

Moses leads the Israelite people in a song of praise to God, after which Miriam appears again. She leads the women in a dance while singing: "Sing to the Lord, for God is highly exalted. Both horse and driver God has hurled into the sea" (Exodus 15:21).

When Miriam is reintroduced in this part of the story, the text refers to her as a "prophetess" (Exodus 15:20), and later in Numbers 12:2 she reveals that God has spoken to her. Later, as the Israelites wander through the desert in search of the Promised Land, the Midrash or Hebrew interpretation tells us that a well of water followed Miriam and quenched the people's thirst.[40]

Miriam was a prophet and leader of the Israelites. Her role and importance, however, have always been overshadowed by Moses.

F. Hagar

We are introduced to Hagar in the book of Genesis 16:1–4 and Genesis 21:8–21. Hagar was a foreigner, a slave, and a woman. Therefore, she was triply oppressed. In normal traditional studies, Hagar was always a negative model because she was rebellious. She wouldn't obey Sarah and was even accused of looking at Sarah with contempt. Hagar was Sarah's slave and as such, served much as a personal maid might today. She could even be given to Abram to bear a child for Sarah (Genesis 16:3).

As the story of Hagar unfolds, she becomes pregnant and looks at Sarah with contempt. Sarah demands that she be demoted from concubine to slave, and Sarah begins to mistreat her. Hagar, who was unwilling to tolerate this abuse, ran away to the desert. There she was visited by an angel of the Lord, who asked her about her past and her future. She replied to the angel that she was fleeing from her cruel mistress. But the angel told her to return to her mistress. It appears here that God was on the side of the oppressors. But perhaps God was ensuring that Hagar and her son would be saved.

Then the angel promised that her descendants would be so numerous that they would not be able to be counted. Hagar is the only woman in the Hebrew scriptures to have such a promise made. We remember that promise to Abram. Customarily that promise is given to the father, but she is the only woman who scriptures state was given that promise. She is also the only woman to have a theophany, a vision of God. For in Genesis 16:13, she asked: "Have I really seen God and remained alive after seeing him?" She gives a name to God—LeRoi—meaning the God of Seeing.

Belonging to a narrative that rejects her, Hagar is a fleeting yet haunting figure in scripture. In many ways, Hagar challenges and shapes faith. Read in the light of contemporary issues and images, her story depicts oppression in three forms: nationality, class, and sex. First, Hagar, the Egyptian, is a maid. Sarah, the Hebrew, is her mistress. Conflicts between these two women revolve around three males. At the center is Abram, their common husband, and to him belong Ishmael, child of Hagar, and Isaac, child of Sarah.

Through their husband and his two sons, these two females clash. From the very beginning, however, Hagar is powerless because God supports Sarah. Kept in her place, the slave woman is the innocent victim of use, abuse, and rejection.

As the symbol of the oppressed, Hagar becomes many things to many people. Most especially, however, all sorts of rejected women find their stories in her. She is the faithful maid who is exploited, the black woman used by the male and abused by the female of the ruling class. The surrogate mother, the resident alien without legal recourse, the other woman, the runaway youth, the pregnant young woman alone, the divorced mother with child, the shopping bag lady carrying bread and water, the homeless woman, the welfare mother, and the self-effacing female whose own identity shrinks in service to others. And besides symbolizing various kinds and conditions of people in society, Hagar is a pivotal figure in biblical theology.

She is, first, the first person in scripture whom a divine messenger visits and the only person who dares to name the deity.

But life was not easy for Hagar and her son Ishmael. When Sarah had a son, Isaac, she became jealous of Hagar and forced Abram to evict "this slave woman with her son." "For the son of a slave woman shall not be heir with my son Isaac" (Genesis 21:10).

Traditional readings of this story overlooked the cruelty and harshness of both Abram and Sarah, hereby insinuating the sins and the feelings of the powerful are somehow to be tolerated to fulfill the will of God. But reading from this perspective of the oppressed allows no such luxury. Abram sent Hagar and Ishmael into the desert only with some bread and a bit of water. When the water had been used up and Hagar could no longer bear to hear the cries of her child, she put him in the shade under a bush and sat a distance from him, because she could not stand to see her son dying.

Once more, God sent an angel to comfort her. But this time the question is not about the past or the future but only about the present. "What troubles you, Hagar? Fear not." God gave comfort and another promise that her son would be father of a great nation. Hagar was put in the traditional role of the father, taking the boy with a strong hand and raising him to be "a wild ass of a man" (Genesis 16:12).

There are a number of parallels between Abram and Hagar. First of all, they both were forced to leave their homes (Genesis 12:1, 21:14). They both received a promise from Yahweh that their descendants would be too numerous to count (Genesis 15:5, 16:10). Each of them was faced with the prospect of a death of a son. Abram was willing to carry it out himself while Hagar could not bear to see her boy die (Genesis 22:9, 21:16, 8).

And finally, they both had theophanies. The Lord appeared to Abram and said "I am the God Almighty or el Shaddai, the God of the Mountains." When the Lord spoke to Hagar, however, it was Hagar who named God. "Thou art the God of Seeing" (16:13).

Through the centuries, Father Abraham the patriarch has been revered and honored and Hagar has been ignored by both Jews and Christians. She is honored by Moslems, however, as the mother of Ishmael. At the time of the pilgrimage in Mecca, they do that in memory of Hagar searching for water to save her son.

Hagar, based on the writing of *Texts of Terror*, is one of the first females in scripture to experience use, abuse, and rejection.[41]

Hagar has been claimed as the patron of homeless people driven from shelter by the powerful even the virtuous powerful. She is also a model for many women left with the responsibility of children by an uncaring father. She complicates the history of salvation and forces us to recognize and condemn the actions of one of Israel's patriarchs.

G. The Named and Unnamed

There are many more women mentioned in the Old Testament. For example:

1. Named

Sarah (Genesis 11:27–32; 12; 13; 16; 17:1–8, 15–21; 18:1–15; 20; 21:1–14; 22:1–14; 24:36, 67:25, 10; Isaiah 51:2): Sarah was the wife of Abraham. She was childless until the age of ninety (26:1–11, 17, 23, 34–35; 27; 28:1–5; 49:29, 31), when she bore a son, Isaac.

Rebekah (Genesis 22:20–13; 24; 25:19–34; 26:1–11, 17, 23, 34–35; 27; 28:1–5;49:29, 31): Rebekah was the wife of Isaac and the mother of Jacob and Esau. She helped her son Jacob conspire against his father to win Esau's birthright and blessing.

Rachel (Genesis 28:1–5; 29:1–31; 30:1–26: 31:4–55; 32:22–24; 33:1–7, 12–14; 35:16–21, 24–25; 46:19–22; 48:7, Jeremiah 31:15): Rachel was Leah's sister, the younger daughter of Rebekah's brother Laban. Jacob worked seven years to win the right to marry her. She is the mother of Joseph and Benjamin.

Hanna (1 Samuel 1:2:1–11, 18–21): Hanna was the wife of Elkanah. She was childless until God heard her intense prayer to become a mother. She gave birth to Samuel whom she consecrated to God, and who became a great prophet.

Shiprah and Puah (Exodus 1:15–22): Shiprah and Puah were Hebrew midwives in Egypt. They defied the orders of Pharaoh to kill all male Hebrew children. They may have delivered Moses. The Hebrew midwives resisted oppression so their people would live.

Ruth and Naomi (the book of Ruth): Ruth was the daughter-in-law of Naomi, who migrated with her family to Moab when famine struck Bethlehem. When Ruth and Naomi both became widowed, Ruth insisted on returning to Bethlehem with Naomi rather than returning to her Moabite people. Ruth married Boaz and was great-grandmother to David.

2. Unnamed

For every woman mentioned in the Bible there are also many who were not named, yet they held a supporting role in the Bible. For example, there were the women who flocked into the streets when David returned home after slaying Goliath.

> It happened as they were coming, when David returned from killing the Philistines that the women came out of all the cities of Israel, singing and dancing, to meet King Saul, with tambourines, with joy and with musical instruments. (1 Samuel 18:6)

There were the women who stood when the Law of Moses was read by Ezra.

And all the people gathered as one man at the square which was in front of the Water Gate, and they asked Ezra the scribe to bring the book of the Law of Moses which the Lord had given to Israel. Then Ezra the priest brought the law before the assembly of men, women and all who could listen with understanding, on the first day of the seventh month. He read from it before the square which was in front of the Water Gate from early morning until midday, in the presence of men and women, those who could understand and all the people were attentive to the book of the law. (Nehemiah 8:1–3)

There were also the "other women" who were present after Christ died.

On the first day of the week, at early dawn, they came to the tomb bringing the spices which they had prepared. (Luke 24:1)

Many of the women who are unnamed are women who are associated with well-known men. For example, the Bible gives the names of the sons of Noah, but not those of his wife and daughters-in-law.

We find a full description of Lot but nothing with regard to the names of his wife and two daughters.

The apostle Peter we know so well from the gospels, but there is no mention of the name of his wife.

The scriptures are silent regarding the identity of many of the women. They played a role in history, but they have no name in the Bible.

Many of these women certainly played a role in history, but their names are omitted.

There are many more that are named and unnamed, used and abused, misunderstood, and ignored and even more who need to be remembered and proclaimed in our churches.

H. Story and Questions to Ponder

Susan graduated in 1989 with a decree in canon law. She was one of thirty graduates that year—four women and twenty-six men. Her class had only been the third graduating class that allowed women in the program, thanks to the changes in the 1983 Code of Canon Law. This was new, novel, and about time. She was appointed judge for the Tribunal in 1989 and had been working there for two years as a member of the Tribunal staff. She was sitting at the lunch table with a priest who was just beginning his canon law degree. He was on summer break, and they were both working at the Tribunal. It was summertime—his first summer as a canon law student and her second year as a canon law graduate.

Another priest came along and sat down next to the two of them. Susan knew this priest since he came often to the Tribunal. At first he did not look at Susan but spoke only to the priest sitting next to her. He said to him, "I need help with a canonical question." Then he turned to Susan and said, "And honey, you can listen if you want."

1. Have you ever been in situations where you felt belittled because of how you were addressed?

2. How did that make you feel? How did you respond to the situation?

3. Have you ever been in a situation where you belittled someone else because of his or her gender or because you felt far superior to him or her?

CHAPTER 6

The Neglected Stories of Women in the Gospels

Besides Mary, the Mother of Jesus, there are nineteen other women mentioned in the gospels. The following passages give us the stories of the women whom Jesus met. Some of them are named, and some are not. They are listed here:

- Elizabeth—Luke 1:5–80
- Anna—Luke 2:36–38
- Woman accused of adultery—John 8:2–11
- Jairus's daughter—Mark 5:21–24, 35–43; Luke 8:40–42; Matthew 9:18–19, 23–26
- Woman with the flow of blood—Mark 5:25–34; Luke 8:43–48; Matthew 9:20–22
- Woman who anoints Jesus's head—Mark 14:3–9; Matthew 26:6–13
- The bent-over woman—Luke 13:10–17
- Poor widow—Mark 12:41–44; Luke 21:1–4
- Canaanite woman – Mark 7:24–30; Matthew 15:21–28
- Herodias and her daughter—Mark 6:17–29; Matthew 14:3–12
- Woman at the well—John 4:1–42
- Mary and Martha—Luke 10:38–42
- Susanna—Luke 8:3

- Johanna—Luke 8:1–3, 24:10
- Mary Magdalene —Luke 8:1–3; John 19:25, 20:1–18; Mark 15:40–41, 47; 16:1–11; Matthew 27:55–56, 61, 28:1–10; Luke 23:49; 55–56; 24:1–11
- Mary, wife of Cleopas—John 19:25; Luke 24:13–53
- Peter's mother-in-law—Luke 4:38–39; Mark 1:29–31; Matthew 8:14–15

At the time of Jesus, women were invisible and powerless with regard to Jewish law and society. As a rule, only rabbis' wives could be educated. Women were not accepted as witnesses in Jewish law, nor could they teach the law. Women had no official religious or leadership roles in first-century Judaism. In a country ruled by the religious elite, this rendered them invisible and powerless—invisible and powerless, that is, to nearly everyone but Jesus.[42] As the gospel shows, Jesus had a special love for those discounted by others. His behavior toward women viewed through the lens of the gospel text is remarkable. Jesus welcomed women into his closest discipleship (Luke 8:1–5). Women were not named in ancient texts unless they had prominence. The clear implication in this text is that wealthy women underwrote the Galilean mission. Jesus welcomed female disciples to learn the ways of God, along with the male disciples. This was highly unusual since women normally didn't speak to men in public, much less travel around the countryside with them. Jesus's radical inclusion of women is also illustrated by the story of Martha and Mary. Mary assumed her place at Jesus's feet, the place traditionally taken by male rabbinical students. Martha protests, but Jesus praises Mary's thirst to learn more about God. (Luke 10:38–42).

A. The Woman at the Well—John 4:1–42

The first passage to examine is the account of the Samaritan woman at the well (John 4:1–42). This woman is not given a name in this gospel passage. However, this may not be unusual in the gospel of John. There are many people in John's gospel who are not given a name. There is the "mother of Jesus." There is no place in the gospel of John where the mother of Jesus is given a name. The gospel of John also refers to John as the "beloved disciple." The gospel also tells the account of the paralyzed man at the pool, the man born blind, and the royal official. These people are real. Perhaps it is possible that the writer of John's gospel wanted to make a point. That point may be that the "nameless" person could be any of us. We are the man born blind, the woman at the well, the paralyzed man. We experience what they experience. We are given a new life because of Jesus. Their story becomes our story. Making them nameless made these stories applicable to all of us.

With the story of the woman at the well, however, the Orthodox Church gives this woman a name. Not only that, they declare her a saint. The name that the Orthodox Church has given her is Saint Photini. Photini means "enlightened one."[43]

This woman carries on a theological discussion with Jesus. Jesus not only carries on a conversation with a Samaritan who is considered a foreigner from a despised religious group but a woman as well.

Jesus and his disciples stop at a roadside well. It is there that Jesus meets a Samaritan woman. They were traveling by way of Samaria. Normally, Jewish travelers would make a detour around Samaria to avoid contact with Samaritans, but Jesus took the direct route.

Jesus made a stop here, tired and thirsty in the midday heat. His friends had gone to the town to buy food. Only a Samaritan woman was there, drawing water from the well.

Every day women would walk this walk, which was not easy. They would fill their heavy jars, carry them up the rock, and then carry their water home. The strong younger women of the household normally did this task, but this is not happening here.

Jesus has nothing to draw water with, so he asks this Samaritan woman for something to drink. Here begins the longest conversation recorded between Jesus and any person in the gospels, and it is with a woman and a non-Jew. She was quite surprised that Jesus spoke to her since it was unusual that Jews and Samaritans would speak to each other.

There had been a long-running conflict between the Jews and the Samaritans. Samaria had been the capital of the northern kingdom of Israel during the period of the divided kingdoms. In 721 BC Assyria conquered Israel and sent most of its people to live in Assyria. The Assyrians replaced the original people with five alien tribes who resettled the area (for information on this event, see 2 Kings 17:13–34).

Eventually many of the original population returned and intermarried with the five alien tribes. By the time of Jesus, Jews thought that the people who lived in Samaria were not true descendants of the great Jewish ancestors and that their religion was not true Judaism but a mixture of beliefs.

But Jesus began talking to this woman about "living water." The woman questioned him and drew him into conversation. Jesus explained that when people drink ordinary water, they get thirsty again. But he had water that gave eternal, not temporary, life.

Naturally this caught the interest of the woman, burdened as she was with the daily task of carrying water. She asked for some of this living water. Jesus told her to go and get her husband. She did not have one, she replied. "You have had five husbands," said Jesus, "but the man you are living with now is not your husband." At this stage the story contains a great deal of symbolism. Jesus uses the word *Baals*, which can be translated as "husbands." But, the word can also be translated as "gods"—which could make more sense in this passage since Jesus would be referring to this Samaritan woman as believing or "having" other gods to worship. This was the big difference in belief between the Jews and the Samaritans. The Samaritans believed in many gods. In fact, the Samaritans believed in five pagan gods, and thus it makes more sense to understand that Jesus is referring to this Samaritans' religious beliefs, not a sexual sin. Of course, when "Baal" is translated as "husband," this immediately leads us to the perception of this woman as a sinner. Let us suppose, as Regina Coll suggests, that Jesus is telling her to ask her god for living water.[44] The main issue of discussion is where to worship. This was a big issue for Jews and Samaritans. And Jesus was already breaking with tradition by saying that where you worship is immaterial. What is important is that you worship in spirit and in truth. Jesus tells her that he has living water to offer, and he who drinks of this water will never thirst.

In this second part of the story, the disciples return. They are hostile to this woman, but she ignores them. She goes back to her town. When she gets there, she tells everyone about Jesus. She brings people to God when she says, "He told me everything I ever did" (John 4:29). Perhaps this doesn't just mean the bad things. Jesus may also have revealed to her all of the good things she has also done. Perhaps he also told her of all the gifts that she has, which no one has ever told her before. And she left her water jar. Her water jar is precious, and she left something valuable. But it also weighed her down because now nothing is as important as the message of Jesus. The disciples urge Jesus to eat, but he says he has already had food.

This woman, who has been depicted as a sinner, instead is revealed as a person who carried on a theological discussion with Jesus.[45] She had a voice, and she moved out into the public arena, into male space. She entered into debate with Jesus about issues and questions that interested her. She did not wait for permission to speak but took the initiative. This woman, whom we can name St. Photini, can teach us many things and can help us examine our relationship with Jesus. Jesus asked this woman for water. He needed something from her.

This leads us to the question: Am I, like this woman, able and willing to share my faith freely and openly with others?

This passage leads us far beyond a story about a sinful woman whom Jesus rebukes because of her many husbands. Instead, it leads us into the longest theological conversation that is recorded in the gospels—a conversation with a woman and a Samaritan. And many believe because of her words. This leads us to the question: what do I need to leave behind so I can concentrate on the message of Jesus? What is slowing me down? What do I need to say no to in order to say yes to the message of Jesus?

B. The Canaanite Woman—Mark 7:24–30

> Jesus got up and went away from there to the region of Tyre. And when He had entered a house, He wanted no one to know of it; yet He could not escape notice. But after hearing of Him, a woman whose little daughter had an unclean spirit immediately came and fell at His feet. Now the woman was a Gentile, of the Syrophoenician race. And she kept asking Him to cast the demon out of her daughter. And He was saying to her, "Let the children be satisfied first, for it is not good to take the children's bread and throw it to the dogs." But she answered and said to Him, "Yes, Lord, but even the dogs under the table feed on the children's crumbs." And He said to her, "Because of this answer—go; the demon has gone out of your daughter." And going back to her home, she found the child lying on the bed, the demon having left.

The lectionary gives no attention at all to this scripture passage. This story tells us about a desperate woman who is not going to give up. Jesus appears to be suffering from burnout. It is the only instance in the scriptures where Jesus does not have the last word. We see, in this passage, the true humanity of Jesus. He is saying that he was sent just to the Jews. Most people see this response by Jesus as saying he was testing her faith. However, this really doesn't make sense in this context. It's not like Jesus to do that, but this passage could be where we see Jesus in his most vulnerable state, where he is suffering from exhaustion, and here is a desperate woman who is not going to give up. It's almost like this woman is saying to Jesus, "Excuse me, but you have a very narrow perspective of God's love. There is enough of God's love to go around to everyone." This is the only instance in the scriptures where Jesus does not have the last word; this woman does, and he learns from her. This is another instance where Jesus is ministered; this is like a passage of mutual ministry. She needs her daughter healed, and he needs his understanding of his ministry broadened, and Jesus here embraces her truth. This woman challenges Jesus, which leaves us with another reflection question: Can I challenge others and accept a challenge from others like Jesus did?

C. The Bent-Over Woman—Luke 13:10–17

> And He was teaching in one of the synagogues on the Sabbath. And there was a woman who for eighteen years had had a sickness caused by a spirit; and she was bent double, and could not straighten up at all. When Jesus saw her, He called her over and said to her, "Woman, you are freed from your sickness." And He laid His hands on her; and immediately she was made erect again and began glorifying God. But the synagogue official, indignant because Jesus had healed on the Sabbath, began saying to the crowd in response, "There are six days in which work should

be done; so come during them and get healed, and not on the Sabbath day." But the Lord answered him and said, "You hypocrites, does not each of you on the Sabbath untie his ox or his donkey from the stall and lead him away to water him? And this woman, a daughter of Abraham as she is, whom Satan has bound for eighteen long years, should she not have been released from this bond on the Sabbath day?" As He said this, all His opponents were being humiliated; and the entire crowd was rejoicing over all the glorious things being done by Him.

The setting for this healing is in the synagogue. Jesus is said to be there as teacher, and so he is teaching in the synagogue. It was there that Jesus saw this woman who was "bent over." Again, here we have a woman in the scriptures who has no name. She has moved through the world for eighteen years, bent over, forced to look down. All she has been able to see for eighteen years is the ground.

Scripture says that she "had a sickness caused by a spirit." In the synoptic gospels, there is a close link between possession of a spirit and illness.

Luke 8:30–39—Possession

And Jesus asked him, "What is your name?" And he said, "Legion"; for many demons had entered him. They were imploring Him not to command them to go away into the abyss. Now there was a herd of many swine feeding there on the mountain; and the demons implored Him to permit them to enter the swine. And He gave them permission. And the demons came out of the man and entered the swine; and the herd rushed down the steep bank into the lake and was drowned.

Luke 9:39—Epilepsy

A spirit seizes him, and he suddenly screams, and it throws him into a convulsion with foaming at the mouth; and only with difficulty does it leave him, mauling him as it leaves."

Luke 11:14—Inability to Speak

And He was casting out a demon, and it was mute; when the demon had gone out, the mute man spoke; and the crowds were amazed.

Because there was such little medical knowledge at that time, often one considered an illness as wrought by some spirit or some mysterious possession. In this passage from Luke 13:10–17, the bent-over woman goes to the synagogue, and Jesus sees her. He calls her over and heals her, and, for the first time in eighteen years, she can see faces instead of the floor. He tells her that she is set free.

This story combines two literary forms in one story.[46] The first is a healing story and a controversy. The controversy is over the Sabbath observance and who has the authority to define what is allowed and not allowed on the Sabbath. The readings of Mark 3:1–6 about the story of the man with a withered hand presents the same controversy. Both are clear in that the answer is that "the Son of Man is Lord of the Sabbath" (Mark 2:28).

When this woman is healed, she, of course, does not stop and consider whether it is the Sabbath. It is a day to give praise and thanks to God—and she does.

Again, similar to the previous story of the Samaritan woman, there is a lesson here for us and a question as well.

- What keeps us bent over? Is it low self-esteem? Is it fear of what others are going to think? Is it anxiety that takes over? What keeps us bent-over?

- Do we have enough faith in the Lord to know that, if we turn to him, he can heal us?

Again, this is another story in the scriptures that isn't just about one woman who was healed, but it is our story as well. The nameless woman could be you, me, or anyone who is not strong enough to stand up straight until the realization comes that Jesus can heal and set us free. Anthony Gittins in his book *Encountering Jesus* suggests that there are "far too many bent-over women in today's church. And, there are some bent-over men as well. They are bent over by the law and its application, by theology and clericalism, by patriarchy and hypocrisy, by a lack of accountability and an obscene abuse of power." He reminds us that this is not the will of God. God's will is that everyone should be able to stand upright and morally straight.[47]

This healing is one of the most empowering stories in the gospel, yet it is read at Mass only once in the three-year cycle of Sunday lectionary readings.

D. Mary of Magdala (Luke 8:1–3; John 19:25; 20:1–18; Mark 15:40–41,47; 16:1–11; Matthew 27:55–56,61; 28:1–10; Luke 23:49; 55–56; 24:1–11)

When studying the scriptures, evidence indicates that Mary of Magdala was among the women who accompanied Jesus on his mission, and she was singled out by Jesus to be the first to see and proclaim him as the risen Christ.

The passage from the Gospel of Luke 8:1–3 tells us that, as Jesus moved from village to village teaching and preaching, he was accompanied by the twelve as well as some women. It mentions here that one of those women was Mary of Magdala from whom seven demons had gone out.

As was stated in an earlier account, the people of Jesus's day believed that spirits and demons caused many illnesses. It was one way of explaining sickness and evil. The gospel states that Mary Magdalene had seven demons tormenting her. The number seven indicated the severity of the illness. There is no indication when Jesus cured her of her illness. In any event, she became the leader of a group of women who traveled with Jesus and who supported him financially. [48]

Two groups traveled with Jesus, a group of men led by Peter, and a group of women led by Mary Magdalene. Unfortunately, the words and actions of the men were recorded, and the women's were not. The other women who went with Mary are also named in the scriptures: Joanna, the wife of Herod's steward (Luke 8:3), and Susanna.

Mary Magdalene is the only woman mentioned by name in all four gospels. The gospels tell us that Mary was a follower of Jesus (Luke 8:2). Scripture also tells us that she was at the foot of the cross and was present when Jesus was buried (Matthew 27:56; 61; John 19:25). She also was the first witness to the resurrection (Matthew 28:1; Mark 16:1, 9; Luke 24:10; John 20:1, 18). She is mentioned in all of the gospel narratives of the resurrection. However, Paul, in his letter to the Corinthians ignores her. He writes, "He appeared to Cephas, then to the twelve, then to the more than five hundred brethren at one time" (1 Corinthians 15:5–6).

Yet, her name has become synonymous with prostitute and harlot. She is remembered as a sinner. And of course, for a woman to be a sinner implies some kind of suspect sexual activity. She is not remembered as a sinner with a sin connected to some kind of injustice or unkindness, but a woman's sin always appears to be sexual. This reputation that she has is a direct response flowing from the statement that she was the woman from whom Jesus had cast out seven demons (Luke 8:2). Yet, we have already noted that, in the synoptic gospels, there is a close link between possession of a spirit and illness. None of the others are labeled as resulting from a sexual sin; the man possessed (Luke 8:30–39), the man with epilepsy (Luke 9:39), and the man who was mute (Luke 11:14). Maybe as Coll aptly states in her book, "the image of a faithful woman who suffered at the crucifixion and to whom Jesus chose to appear before all others seems to be more than a patriarchal society could comprehend."[49]

Early church fathers helped in developing the idea of Mary as the sinful woman. Reading the homilies of Gregory the Great, who was pope from AD 590 to 604 "sealed her fate."[50] In his homilies Pope Gregory identifies Mary as the sinful woman, and he continues by explaining the seven demons that possessed her represented the seven capital sins.[51]

Mary of Magdala is also described by some as "apostle to the apostles," or even the first apostle. However, what does that say about the apostolic line—that is, the church's teaching regarding Holy Orders? As the Catholic Catechism states: "Holy Orders is the Sacrament of the apostolic ministry. It is for bishops, as successors of the apostles to so hand on the gift of the spirit." [52] Yet Rome still insists that the Lord chose only men to form the "college of apostles" and that this apostolic succession structures the whole liturgical life of the church.[53]

Yet—wouldn't it be only fair to say that, according to the scriptures, Mary Magdalene was the first of the apostles? She was the leader of the women apostles who did not abandon Jesus at the cross, as was stated about the men apostles. In fact, one of the most moving accounts in scripture is the account of the women at the tomb.

The Congregation for Divine Worship and the Discipline of the Sacraments has issued a decree raising the obligatory memorial of St. Mary Magdalene, celebrated on July 22, to the dignity of a feast. In its decree, dated June 3, 2016, and released on June 10, the Congregation has published a new proper Latin preface for the feast that will be translated into other languages. The decree states that in our time, the Church is called to a more profound reflection, "on the dignity of women, the new evangelization, and the abundance of the mystery of divine mercy, all of which are manifest in the life of the saint."[54]

Archbishop Arthur Roche, the Congregation's secretary, said the decree was issued in response to the expressed desire of Pope Francis. It is fitting, the prelate added, that St. Mary Magdalene—described by St. Thomas Aquinas and others as the "apostle of the apostles"—is now commemorated with a liturgical feast, as the apostles are.[55]

E. The Women at the Last Supper

So—were the women followers of Jesus invited to dine with Jesus for his last Passover meal? Matthew, Mark, and Luke's gospel all begin their story of the Last Supper by telling us that Jesus wanted to share the Passover with his disciples.

> Now on the first day of Unleavened Bread the disciples came to Jesus and asked, "Where do you want us to prepare for you to eat the Passover?" And He said, "Go into the city to a certain man, and say to him, 'The Teacher says, "My time is near; I am to keep the Passover at your house with my disciples."' The disciples did as Jesus had directed them; and they prepared the Passover. (Matthew 26:17–19)

> On the first day of Unleavened Bread, when the Passover lamb was being sacrificed, His disciples said to Him, "Where do you want us to go and prepare for you to eat the Passover?" And He sent

two of His disciples and said to them, "Go into the city, and a man will meet you carrying a pitcher of water; follow him; and wherever he enters, say to the owner of the house, 'The Teacher says, "Where is My guest room in which I may eat the Passover with My disciples?" And he himself will show you a large upper room furnished and ready; prepare for us there. .The disciples went out and came to the city, and found it just as He had told them; and they prepared the Passover. (Mark 14:12–26)

Then came the first day of Unleavened Bread on which the Passover lamb had to be sacrificed. And Jesus sent Peter and John, saying, "Go and prepare the Passover for us, so that we may eat it." They said to Him, "Where do you want us to prepare it?" And He said to them, "When you have entered the city, a man will meet you carrying a pitcher of water; follow him into the house that he enters. And you shall say to the owner of the house, 'The Teacher says to you, "Where is the guest room in which I may eat the Passover with My disciples? "And he will show you a large, furnished upper room; prepare it there." And they left and found everything just as He had told them; and they prepared the Passover. (Luke 22:7–13)

While all three gospels note that there was a special place at the table for the apostles, that does not mean that the last supper was only with the apostles. What is important to note is that the gospels do not restrict attendance at the Last Supper to just this group.

Immediately after the section about who was at Jesus's table, the three evangelists tell us about Jesus's "words over the bread and the wine." Matthew, however, is the only one of the evangelists who directly answers the question of whether Jesus said the Eucharistic words to all his disciples or only to the twelve at his table. Using almost the same words as the consecration of the Mass, Matthew explicitly states that Jesus addressed the words over the bread to his disciples.

> While they were eating, Jesus took some bread, and after a blessing, He broke it and gave it to the disciples, and said, "Take, eat; this is my body." And when He had taken a cup and given thanks, He gave it to them, saying, "Drink from it, all of you; this is my blood of the covenant, which is poured out for many for forgiveness of sins. But I say to you, I will not drink of this fruit of the vine from now on until that day when I drink it new with you in My Father's kingdom." (Matthew 25:25)

Like the three evangelists, John also supports the idea that there were other disciples besides the twelve in the room where the Last Supper was held. John uses only the word *disciples*, never apostles or the twelve. Jesus washes the feet of his disciples, he shares food with his disciples, and he gives his final discourse to the disciples.

The earliest form of liturgy that includes the words of consecration is the anaphora of Basil of Caesarea from about AD 357. It uses both words *disciples* and *apostles*. It states, "Jesus took bread, blessed, sanctified, broke and gave it to his holy disciples and apostles ..." These words are still being used in the Coptic and Orthodox liturgies.[56]

That is the same with the liturgy from the church at Antioch, which is attributed to St. Clement of Rome. It is preserved in book 8 of the Apostolic Constitutions, compiled in about the fourth century. At the consecration, this liturgy says that Jesus broke the bread "and gave it to his disciples." Since that liturgy also uses the word *apostles* elsewhere, the use of the word *disciples* at the consecration must have been intentional.[57]

The next time you attend Mass, pay attention to the words of the priest at the time of consecration: "On the night he was betrayed Jesus said to his disciples." The word used very clearly is disciple, not apostle. It is most likely that we have been hearing what artists trained us to hear in their drawings of the Last Supper, showing Jesus sitting at the table with twelve men. But scripture and tradition do not support the idea that only the twelve male apostles were at the Last Supper.[58] Interesting, isn't it? This time the women were invited, and they showed up as well—but strange how we have been led to believe that they were not worthy enough to be invited …

F. The Women at the Crucifixion

Suggested scripture passages: Mark 15:40–41,47;16:1–8; Matthew 27:55–61; 28:1–10; Luke 23:49–56; 24:1–12; John 19:25–27; 20:1–3, 10–18).

The women mentioned in these passages are the Galilean women at the cross and at the tomb. These women have been with Jesus from the very beginning of his ministry. The story of their travels and their fidelity to Jesus cuts across all four gospel accounts. Also, all four gospels place women at the tomb to become the first witnesses to the resurrection. Yet, at the same time the four gospels vary as to who the women were who accompanied Jesus to the cross and to his burial.

Mark names three women at the cross: Mary Magdalene; Mary, the mother of the younger James and Joses; and Salome (Mark 14:40, 16:1).

Matthew tell us that at the cross were "Mary Magdalene and Mary the mother of James and Joseph, and the mother of the sons of Zebedee" (Matthew 27:56). A few verses later (v. 61) Matthew says that two of these, "Mary Magdalene and the other Mary remained sitting there, facing the tomb."

Luke describes the woman as those who "had followed him from Galilee" (Luke 23:49) and named them as Mary Magdalene, Joanna, and Mary the mother of James (Luke 24:10).

In John's gospel we are told that "standing by the cross of Jesus were his mother and his mother's sister, Mary, the wife of Clopas, and Mary of Magdala" (John 19:25).

These women who accompany Jesus throughout his ministry also accompany him to his death. These women disciples did not run away or abandon him. They kept vigil. Matthew 26:56 makes the point to tell us that all the male disciples deserted Jesus and fled for their lives. But the women remained, standing as near as they dared to the spot where the soldiers were carrying out the brutal execution. Certainly, for the men it was more dangerous for them to be near the execution site. The Romans saw Jesus as a dangerous rebel leader, so they viewed Jesus's male friends with suspicion. Women were seen as less threatening, so their presence was tolerated. The presence of the women at the tomb was meant to highlight the factual nature of the burial—that Jesus was indeed dead, and that his body had been buried in the normal manner.

This point was later disputed by people who said that Jesus had not been dead, but merely unconscious. Since women's testimony was not given the same weight as men's in courts of law, this might have been a problem. Deuteronomy 19:15 stipulated that at least two or three witnesses were needed to prove that something had happened.

But the gospels also stress that Joseph of Arimathea, a respected member of the council, was also there, so the required number of witnesses was present at the tomb of Jesus to verify that he was really dead.

Matthew, Mark, and Luke all tell us that the women who had come from Galilee followed, and they saw the tomb and how Jesus's body was laid. They left, only to return with the properly prepared spices and ointments (Luke 23:55–56, Mark 15:47, Matthew 27:61). And because they knew where his tomb was, they were the first to discover it empty. They went to the tomb and discovered that the stone had been rolled away.

G. The Women at the Empty Tomb

There is no doubt that stones are a powerful image in the scriptures.

> The stone that was rejected by you, the builders ... has become the cornerstone. (Acts 4:11)

> As for these things that you see, the days will come when there will not be left here one stone upon another that will not be thrown down. (Luke 21:6)

> As you come to him, a living stone rejected by men but in the sight of God chosen and precious. (1 Peter 2:4)

> You are Peter, and upon this rock I will build my church. (Matthew 16:18)

> Whichever one of you has committed no sin may throw the first stone at her. (John 8:7)

> As for these things that you see, the days will come when there will not be left here one stone upon another that will not be thrown down. (Luke 21:6)

The gospel of Mark tells us that the women wanted to anoint the body of Jesus after his death; the stone in front of the tomb was going to be their obstacle to accomplishing this mission. One can imagine those women rushing to the tomb to anoint the body of Jesus—all the while, they were wondering who would move the stone for them. This is a big obstacle, I mean a monumental obstacle, which would take at least sixteen Roman guards to move. But this did not stop them from going to the tomb to anoint his body.

> When the Sabbath was over, Mary Magdalene, and Mary the mother of James, and Salome bought spices, so that they might go and anoint him. And very early on the first day of the week, when the sun had risen, they went to the tomb. They had been saying to one another, "Who will roll away the stone for us from the entrance to the tomb?" When they looked up, they saw that the stone, which was very large, had already been rolled back. (Mark 16:1–4)

How did that happen? Who rolled the stone away? That was no small matter. In Jesus's day, such tombs were usually in a depression, and the stone was rolled down an incline to cover the mouth of the tomb. For a small grave, about twenty men were required to roll a stone down a hill to cover the door of the tomb. Thus, to roll the stone away, the women would have needed more than a full Roman guard. The stone was certainly going to be an obstacle to their getting to Jesus to anoint his body. So—what a surprise it was for them to arrive there and find that the stone had been rolled away.

In Matthew's account, there was an earthquake and an angel who descended from heaven to open the tomb. There are no such dramatics in Mark's telling, though his version is no less powerful. Mark says, "When they looked up, they saw that the stone which was very large, had already been rolled back" (Mark 16:4). Mark uses the Greek word *anakekulistai*, which is perfect passive: "has been rolled away." Very often, when a verb in the passive voice is used in scripture, it has only one meaning. God is the agent. We see this repeated in the writings of Paul and in the use of the passive verb in the beatitudes. Pious Jews would regularly use the passive to avoid using the name of God, because God's name was too holy to say out loud. So, ultimately Mark makes it all too clear—the stone at the door of the tomb has been rolled away because God rolled it away.

The women had to have known that they would be unable to move the stone, but they went anyway. They took it on faith that they could gain access to the tomb, even if they didn't know how. What a lesson for us. The women had enough faith to trust that God would take care of the obstacles.

H. Mary, the Mother of God and Our Sister

There is probably no woman in history who has generated as much attention as the Blessed Virgin Mary. She has been the subject of thousands of paintings, poems, prayers, and even titles. She has been called the Queen of Peace, the Black Madonna, the Mother of Perpetual Help, Our Lady of Guadeloupe, the Blessed Mother, the Mother of Mercy, the Immaculate Conception, Our Lady of the Miraculous Medal, Theotokos, and so many more.

This last title, Theotokos, perhaps is the most unfamiliar to us. *Theotokos,* the word coming from Greek Orthodoxy, means "God-Bearer." This title, defined by the Council of Ephesus in AD 431, refers to the Virgin Mary as the Mother of the Incarnate Son of God. This council was called because of the doctrine of Nestorianism, which emphasized the distinction between Christ's human nature and divine nature. It was argued that Mary should be called Christotokos, which means Christ-bearer, and not Theotokos, which means God-bearer. The council in fact condemned the teachings of Nestorius as heresy and declared Mary as God-bearer. [59]

With all of these titles given to Mary, it makes perfect sense that St. Anthony Messenger Press would publish an article called "In Search of the Real Mary."[60]

In this article, written by Elizabeth Johnson, she states that each one of the gospel writers gives us a different picture of who this woman is, reflecting their unique and very different theologies. For example, Mark points to the passage about Mary in 3:31–35.

> Then, his mother and his brothers arrived, and standing outside they sent word to Him and called Him. A crowd was sitting around Him, and they said to Him," Behold, Your mother and your brothers are outside looking for you." Answering them, He said, "Who are my mother and my brothers? Looking about at those who were sitting around Him, He Said, "Behold, my mother and my brothers! For whoever does the will of God, he is my brother and sister and mother."

In this passage Mark does not seem to have a positive view of Mary. For Mark, Mary remains "outside."

Matthew's view of Mary is pretty neutral. She is placed in the genealogy of Jesus, in line with four other women who act outside the patriarchal marriage structure. What is interesting here is that the story of Jesus's birth is concentrated on Joseph, not on Mary. Mary has no voice in the gospel of Matthew.

> Now the birth of Jesus Christ took place in this way. When his mother Mary had been betrothed to Joseph, before they came together she was found to be with child from the Holy Spirit. And her husband, Joseph, being a just man and unwilling to put her to shame, resolved to divorce her quietly. But as he considered these things, behold, an angel of the Lord appeared to him in a dream, saying," Joseph, son of David, do not fear to take Mary as your wife, for that which is conceived in her is from the Holy Spirit. She will bear a son, and you shall call his name Jesus, for he will save his people from

their sins. All this took place to fulfill what the Lord had spoken by the prophet: Behold the virgin shall conceive and bear a son, and they shall call his name 'Immanuel". Which means God with us. When Joseph woke from sleep, he did as the angel of the Lord commanded him: he took his wife, but knew her not until she had given birth to a so. And he called his name Jesus. (Matthew 1:18–25)

In Luke's gospel, Mary is revealed to us as a great woman of faith. She is the one who "hears the Word of God, and keeps it." It is from the gospel of Luke that we have gotten most of our traditional understanding of who Mary is. We learn, from Luke, that her hometown is Nazareth (Luke 1:26), and we learn about some of her relatives (Elizabeth, for example in Luke 1:5, 1:36). It is in this gospel that we have the longest set of words placed on the lips of any woman in the New Testament—the Magnificat (Luke 1:46–55). She is a loving mother who travels to Bethlehem, gives birth to Jesus, wraps him in swaddling clothes, and places him in a manger (Luke 2:19, 2:51). Luke even reveals her state of mind, stating that she treasured in her heart the things that had happened (Luke 2:19, 2:51).

There is no infancy narrative in the gospel of John, but Mary plays a very important role. She was present when Jesus turned water into wine at the wedding feast at Cana (John 2:1–11). John also places her as a witness to the crucifixion (John 19:25). It is also at the cross where Mary and the "beloved disciple" are called into a mutual relationship (John 19:26–27)

In John, again, Mary does not have a name. Every account in John refers to Mary as the mother of Jesus. John never names her.

In any case, Mary is a great role model for all believers. Mary has been called our mother, the mother of God, the mother of Jesus. But she has also been called our sister in faith, which is a title of a book about her, written by Elizabeth Johnson. She is truly our mother of faith, and our sister in faith as well. Many women might feel alienated from Mary because traditional piety presents her as a timid, submissive woman. That was the image that was formed by previous generations who drew on their own cultural norms regarding women. But over the years, there has formed a new understanding of Mary. Pope Paul VI describes Mary as strong and intelligent—one who even had the courage to question when the angel addressed her, one who experienced poverty and suffering, flight and exile. In the midst of all these troubles, she consistently gave active and responsible consent to the call of God. Rather than being submissively pious, she was a woman who did not hesitate to proclaim that God vindicates the humble and the oppressed.[61] As women today grow to appreciate themselves better, they then can see and understand and appreciate Mary more than ever before. Women can now speak because of Mary who spoke with authority because the authority that women speak from is the Spirit of God.

I. Story and Questions to Ponder

Mary, Our Mother and Protector

Sharon was only ten years old, but she felt pretty experienced for one so young. After all, she knew laughter and grief. But she didn't know that it was grief she was feeling, because she knew how to play a lot of make-believe.

Make believe that you are not frightened. Keep pretending and all will be well.

She learned at a young age that courage only comes when conquering episodes of fear.

She learned that love and pain ... can sometimes feel the same.

Sharon had a sister who was a year older than she was. But despite the one-year age difference, they did everything together. They sang together, played monopoly together, and played hopscotch together.

They played with Lucky, the neighbor's dog.

Sometimes they would dress up and pretend they were movie stars. Other times they would set up an altar and pretend they were altar boys serving Father at Mass. (*This was long before altar girls were allowed!*)

They loved, laughed, cried ...

And tried to hide their pain.

Their world was frightening. But they were too young to know how frightening it really was.

They shared the same bedroom, and tonight it was time for sleep. It was quiet, and Sharon went into the other room to look for her nightgown. It was a still moment, and she heard a beautiful voice call her name. Then, the voice was gone. But it was a call from somewhere beyond her world. She knew that—and from that moment on, she knew that the *voice* was the voice of the Blessed Mother. She did not know why she knew that. But she knew it with certainty—and she knew, from that moment on that there was no reason to fear.

She went to tell her sister. She found her sister waiting for her because her sister wanted to tell her that something had just happened to her. She sat Sharon down, and said to her, "When you were in the other room, I was just sitting here, when suddenly I heard a voice—a beautiful lady's voice, and she called my name. I knew in an instant that it was the *voice* of the Blessed Mother, and I felt safe. I felt that everything is going to be okay."

Sharon then told her that she heard the same voice call her name as well.

They each held out their hand for the other to hold. They knew then that Mary was truly their mother and she would look after them.

The Blessed Mother would keep them safe.

Mary is a model for all of us—her bravery, her faith, her steadfastness gives us courage—the woman who can truly be for us, our stronghold and protector.

1. What quality of Mary do you find most attractive, and what quality would you want most to emulate in your own life?

2. If you were to choose a title or name for Mary, which one best describes Mary for you?

3. Do you have a favorite prayer or hymn of Mary that you would like to share with others?

CHAPTER 7

When in Doubt, Leave Them Out

As has been noted so far, women have played a major role in redemption history. They have also been incredible role models in answering the call of Jesus to live and serve the gospel message. Yet, despite many of these women's incredible journeys of faith and heroism, they have often been ignored and left out when the stories of faith and heroism have been recounted. This same neglect is apparent when it comes to the lectionary readings for Sunday and weekday Mass.

The revision of the lectionary was mandated by the Constitution on the Sacred Liturgy, one of the documents that resulted from the Second Vatican Council. This new lectionary took effect on Palm Sunday, 1970. After a critical look at the lectionary, one will notice that a disproportionate number of passages about the women of the Bible have been omitted or ignored. Let's examine some of those passages as examples of this neglect.

A. Shiphrah and Puah—Exodus 1:8–22

Now a new king arose over Egypt, who did not know Joseph. He said to his people, "Behold, the people of the sons of Israel are more and mightier than we. Come, let us deal wisely with them, or else they will multiply and in the event of war, they will also join themselves to those who hate us, and fight against us and depart from the land." So they appointed taskmasters over them to afflict them with hard labor. And they built for Pharaoh Storage cities, Pithom and Raamses. But the more they afflicted them, the more they multiplied and the more they spread out, so that they were in dread of the sons of Israel. The Egyptians compelled the sons of Israel to labor rigorously; and they made their lives bitter with hard labor in mortar and bricks and at all kinds of labor in the field, all their labors which they rigorously imposed on them. Then the king of Egypt spoke to the Hebrew midwives, one of whom was named Shiphrah and the other was named Puah; and he said, "When you are helping the Hebrew women to give birth and see them upon the birth stool, if it is a son, then you shall put him to death; but if it is a daughter, then she shall live. But the midwives feared God, and did not do as the king of Egypt had commanded them, but let the boys live. So the king of Egypt called for the midwives and said to them, "Why have you done this thing, and let the boys live?" The midwives said to Pharaoh, "Because the Hebrew women are not as the Egyptian women; for they are vigorous and give birth before the midwife can get to them." So God was good to the midwives, and the people multiplied, and became very mighty. Because the midwives feared God, He established households for them. Then Pharaoh commanded all his people, saying, "Every son who is born you are to cast into the Nile, and every daughter you are to keep alive."

This reading from the book of Exodus is proclaimed on Monday of the fifteenth week of Ordinary Time, Year One, except the section in red print (verses 14–22). That section is the story of Shiphrah and Puah, two brave midwives. In this story these two women risk their own lives by defying the pharaoh's law of death to uphold God's law of life. They refused Pharaoh's order, which was to kill all male Hebrew children. Had they obeyed him, Moses would never have grown to adulthood. What wonderful role models for following God and conscience rather than the death-dealing laws of the state.

Their heroic story is not read, but instead, skipped. The reading goes from Exodus 1:8–14, then verses 14–22 are skipped, and then it ends with verse 22.

B. Deborah—Judges 5:1–31

Deborah is named a prophet and judge of Israel. When she was judge of Israel, it had been under severe oppression for twenty years. But as Judge, she planned a military strategy against the Canaanites, appointed a general, and led a victorious battle. Her song of victory is found in Judges 5:1–31 and is considered to be one of the most ancient compositions of the Bible. Even though this story is of incredible bravery, it is never read in the Sunday or daily lectionary readings at Mass. What is read are the stories of Gideon, Jephthah, and Samson, as well as the two sons of Samuel. But the only female judge, renowned for her bravery, is never read at weekday or Sunday liturgies. She is left "standing at the gate."[62]

C. Huldah

On Wednesday of the twelfth week in Ordinary Time we hear the reading from 2 Kings 22:8–13, 23:1–3.

> Then Hilkiah the high priest said to Shaphan the scribe, "I have found the book of the law in the house of the Lord." And Hilkiah gave the book to Shaphan who read it. Shaphan the scribe came to the king and brought back word to the king and said, "Your servants have emptied out the money that was found in the house, and have delivered it into the hand of the workmen who have the oversight of the house of the Lord." Moreover, Shaphan the scribe told the king saying, "Hilkiah the priest has given

me a book." And Shaphan read it in the presence of the king. When the king heard the words of the book of the law, he tore his clothes. Then the king commanded Hilkiah the priest, Ahikam the son of Shaphan, Achbor the son of Micaiah, Shaphan the scribe, and Asaiah the king's servant saying, "Go, inquire of the Lord for me and the people and all Judah concerning the words of this book that has been found, for great is the wrath of the Lord that burns against us, because our fathers have not listened to the words of this book, to do according to all that is written concerning us." So Hilkiah the priest, Ahikam, Achbor, Shaphan, and Asaiah went to Huldah the prophetess, the wife of Shallum the son of Tikvah, the son of Harhas, keeper of the wardrobe (now she lived in Jerusalem in the Second Quarter); and they spoke to her. She said to them, "Thus says the LORD God of Israel, 'Tell the man who sent you to me, thus says the LORD, "Behold, I bring evil on this place and on its inhabitants, even all the words of the book which the king of Judah has read. Because they have forsaken Me and have burned incense to other gods that they might provoke Me to anger with all the work of their hands, therefore My wrath burns against this place, and it shall not be quenched."' But to the king of Judah who sent you to inquire of the LORD thus shall you say to him, 'Thus says the LORD God of Israel, "Regarding the words which you have heard, because your heart was tender and you humbled yourself before the LORD when you heard what I spoke against this place and against its inhabitants that they should become a desolation and a curse, and you have torn your clothes and wept before

Me, I truly have heard you," declares the LORD. Then the king sent, and they gathered to him all the elders of Judah and of Jerusalem. The king went up to the house of the LORD and all the men of Judah and all the inhabitants of Jerusalem with him, and the priests and the prophets and all the people, both small and great; and he read in their hearing all the words of the book of the covenant which was found in the house of the LORD. The king stood by the pillar and made a covenant before the LORD, to walk after the LORD, and to keep His commandments and His testimonies and His statutes with all his heart and all his soul, to carry out the words of this covenant that were written in this book. And all the people entered into the covenant.

Verses 15–19 refer to Huldah, the prophet, one of the very few female prophets mentioned in the Bible. When an old scroll was found in the temple by the priest, Hilkiah, the king ordered, "Go, inquire of the LORD for me and the people and all Judah concerning the words of this book that has been found, for great is the wrath of the LORD that burns against us, because our fathers have not listened to the words of this book, to do according to all that is written concerning us" (2 Kings 22:13). The royal delegation took the scroll not to Jeremiah but to Huldah, who verified the authenticity of the scroll and, as a prophet, spoke God's warnings to the king. However, on Wednesday, the twelfth week in Ordinary Time, the reading from 2 Kings 22:8–13; 23:1–3 is read. But the section above (vv. 15–19), right in the middle of the text, is excised from the reading.

D. Esther

The book of Esther gives us the story of the Jewish people who stayed behind after most returned to Jerusalem after captivity. Babylon had been conquered by Persia and Esther becomes the queen to Ahasuerus of Persia. She was personally chosen by the king. "The king loved Esther more than all the women, and she found favor and kindness with him" (2:17), probably because of her beauty and intelligence.

Mordecai, who is Esther's guardian, refused to bow down and pay homage to Haman, who is a high official of the king. Haman is so angered, and he then vows to destroy all the Jews in the kingdom. Mordecai hears of the plot and reports this to Esther. "For if you remain silent at this time, relief and deliverance will arise for the Jews from another place and you and your father's house will perish. And who knows whether you have not attained royalty for such a time as this?" (4:14).

From chapters 5–10, Esther outwits Haman and takes her petition to the king and begs for the protection of her Jewish people from Haman's wicked stratagem. The king, out of anger, has Haman hung on the gallows, which he had built to destroy all the Jews. Esther's faith and courage save her people.

However, her story is only proclaimed in a Lenten weekday reading that records her prayer appealing to God for strength. No account of the bravery with which she saved her people from annihilation is given anywhere else in the lectionary. Three other passages from the book of Esther are found in the lectionary (in the Common of Saints, #737; and in Masses for Various Occasions, #821, #876), and all three are accounts of the prayer of Esther's uncle, Mordecai.

E. Phoebe

There is a preponderance of evidence that depicts women in ministry as *diakonos* and later, as deaconesses. One of the most famous and earliest examples comes to us from Romans 16:1–2. Here Paul writes: "I commend to you our sister Phoebe, who is a (diakonos) servant of the church which is at Cenchrea; that you receive her in the Lord in a manner worthy of the saints." In Phoebe there is evidence that women were traveling missionaries, deacons, and leaders, whose authority and importance were recognized by Paul as well as by Christian communities.

Take note that the word *diakonos* in other places in scripture, when it refers to a male, is translated as deacon. Mary Ann Getty-Sullivan points out in her book *Women in the New Testament,* that in this passage, when referring to "our sister, Phoebe," it is translated as servant or minister. [63]

The New American Bible does not translate *diakonos* as "deacon" when used to describe Phoebe. Instead, it translates the word as "minister," which is more a generic term that can more easily suggest a subordinate function considered proper for a woman. Mary Ann Getty-Sullivan continues by saying, "These sleights of pen illustrate that a translation is an interpretation and that an androcentric bias has been at work in the reading of the biblical texts for a long time."

F. Miriam

There are passages in the Bible where women are not so much overlooked or excised from the lectionary readings, as much as positive references regarding them are omitted while the negative references are retained. For example, in Exodus 15:20–21 we read where Miriam, the sister of Moses and Aaron is identified as a prophet and leads a liturgy of thanksgiving after the crossing of the sea. "Miriam the prophetess, Aaron's sister, took the timbrel in her hand, and all the women went out after her with timbrels and with dancing. Miriam answered them, "Sing to the LORD, for He is highly exalted; The horse and his rider He has hurled into the sea.'" This passage is omitted from the lectionary. Instead, what is read at the Easter Vigil is the account of Moses leading the song of victory, not Miriam, which most scholars now say was borrowed from the Miriam story, which is the older scriptural tradition. Miriam's weaker side, however, is revealed later, in the story of her envy and punishment with leprosy (Numbers 12:1–13) in a weekday reading (Tuesday of the eighteenth week in Ordinary Time, Year I, #408)

G. Magnificat—Luke 1:46–56

One of the most beautiful passages in the Gospel is the Magnificat.
And Mary said:

> "My soul exalts the Lord,
> And my spirit has rejoiced in God my Savior.
> For He has had regard for the humble state of His
> bond slave;
> For behold, from this time on all generations will
> count me blessed.
> For the Mighty One has done great things for me;
> And holy is His name.
> And His mercy is UPON generation after generation
> Toward those who fear Him.
> He has done mighty deeds with His arm;
> He has scattered those who were proud in the
> thoughts of their heart.
> He has brought down rulers from their thrones,
> And has exalted those who were humble.
> He has filled the hungry with good things;
> And sent away the rich empty-handed.
> He has given help to Israel His servant,

> In remembrance of His mercy,
> As He spoke to our fathers,
> To Abraham and his descendants forever."

This beautiful song is never proclaimed on a Sunday. It is read on a weekday before Christmas as well as on two feast days of Mary, the feast of the Visitation and the feast of the Assumption. But many Catholics will never hear this reading since it is never proclaimed on a Sunday.

H. The Risen Christ Meets Mary Magdalene—John 20:11–18

For the Easter Sunday reading from the lectionary, we hear proclaimed the gospel of John where Peter and the "other disciple" found the empty tomb and "they believed" (John 20:1–9). But if that passage was continued, we would hear the beautiful reading about Mary Magdalene where Jesus appears to her in the garden and says,

> Do not hold on to me, for I have not yet ascended to the Father. Go instead to my brothers and tell them, "I am ascending to my Father and your Father, to my God and your God." Mary Magdalene went to the disciples with the news: "I have seen the Lord!" And she told them that he had said these things to her.

This beautiful story where the risen Lord appears to Mary Magdalene is never proclaimed on a Sunday. But the section right before the appearance to Mary Magdalene, (John 20:1–7) and the section right after (John 20:19–31) is proclaimed on Easter Sunday and second Sunday of Easter. Her beautiful story is skipped.

I. Mary of Bethany

In the gospel of John, the anointing of Jesus is performed by Mary of Bethany at a banquet served by her sister Martha.

> Jesus, therefore, six days before the Passover, came to Bethany where Lazarus was, whom Jesus had raised from the dead. So they made Him a supper there, and Martha was serving; but Lazarus was one of those reclining at the table with Him. Mary then took a pound of very costly perfume of pure nard, and anointed the feet of Jesus and wiped His feet with her hair; and the house was filled with the fragrance of the perfume. But Judas Iscariot, one of His disciples, who was intending to betray Him, said, "Why was this perfume not sold for three hundred denarii and given to poor people?" Now he said this, not because he was concerned about the poor, but because he was a thief, and as he had the money box, he used to pilfer what was put into it. Therefore Jesus said, "Let her alone, so that she may keep it for the day of My burial. For you always have the poor with you, but you do not always have Me.

This version of the anointing story (John 12:1–8) is read only on a weekday, on Monday of Holy Week. It is not included in the reading of the Passion on Good Friday, which is taken from the gospel of John.

J. Holy Family Sunday

Holy Family Sunday occurs the Sunday after Christmas. One would expect, on this day, to find readings that depict the Holy Family as a model for today's families. The first reading from the book of Sirach does offer respect for both mothers and fathers (Sirach 3:4): "He who honors his father atones for sin. He stores up riches who reveres his mother." However, the following responsorial psalm (Psalm 128) appears to be addressed to men and reflects the psalmist view of what woman should be: "Your wife shall be like a fruitful vine in the recesses of your home." The second reading is of the same vein: "You who are wives, be submissive to your husbands" (Colossians 3:18). On a positive note, however, the US bishops requested and received permission from the Vatican in June of 1992 to omit that verse and the following three verses from public readings. A similar request and permission was received to also shorten Ephesians 5:21–32 to omit, "Wives, should be submissive to their husbands ..." on the twenty-first Sunday in Ordinary Time, Year B.[64]

K. Calendar of the Saints

An important part of our Catholic experience is the remembrance and celebration of the saints of the church. From the time of the early martyrs, saints have been brought to our attention for veneration, examples to follow, and encouragement in our own lives of prayer and service.

The saints are considered our spiritual guides, our companions on our journey toward holiness. It is quite a process to be formally recognized as a saint by the Catholic Church. The history of sainthood in the Catholic church began in 993 when Pope John XV elevated Uric of Augsburg formally and universally as we do today, to the level of a saint. Before that time, local bishops would decide which candidates would have honorable mention and feast days. Originally, only martyrs were honored and "recommended" to the public. Pope Alexander III in the twelfth century was the first pope to restrict the prerogative of canonization to the Holy See. In 1983 the process was modified. The person must have died at least five years prior to the beginning of the process. There are three levels in the process for being proclaimed a saint.[65]

The first level is the call to be *venerable*. The congregation researches the candidate's virtues to verify if the person practiced virtue to a heroic degree, or died a martyr's death, and either does or does not recommend their cause. When the pope accepts the report, the candidate is termed "venerable."

Blessed: The second stage is entered. This is a very lengthy process of scrutiny over the person's life, virtues, writings, and reputation for holiness. Customarily one miracle must be credited to the candidate's intercession with God. The venerable candidate would then be "beatified" by the pope at a ceremony in St. Peter's Basilica.

Saint: Canonization means being "raised to the full honors of the altar." A second miracle after beatification is required. In the ceremonies, the name of the saint is mentioned in the Eucharistic prayer of the Mass, and is usually accorded triduum, often in another church in Rome.[66]

The present lectionary of readings for the weekday and Sunday Mass follows the revised calendar. But the revised sanctoral cycle has an unbalanced ratio of 144 male saints to 18 female saints. (The US bishops have since added ten men and seven women to the roster.) The month of June alone brings nineteen men before the church for veneration and no women. Days within the sanctoral cycle are ranked in the order of solemnity, feast, memorial, and optional memorial. The celebrations in honor of Mary, Joseph, John the Baptist, Peter, and Paul are given the status of solemnities. Feasts are also assigned to these five again, as well as to fourteen men. The highest rank in the calendar that any woman besides Mary has achieved is that of memorial. Even though Mary Magdalene has been recognized through the centuries as "apostle to the apostles," she still had ranked below the twelve in the liturgy up until just recently when Pope Francis had her elevated to a feast.[67]

Memorials of both men and women saints use both the Common of Martyrs and the Common of Saints. But only memorials of men use the Common of Pastors and the Common of Doctors. Only memorials of women are assigned to the Common of Virgins, even though many of the male saints are in fact virgins as well.

The memorials of the only two women ever named "doctors" of the church—Catherine of Siena and Teresa of Avila—each do have proper first readings, but the gospel is chosen not from the Common of Doctors but from the Common of Virgins (for both Catherine and Teresa) or the Common of Saints.[68]

L. Women as Martyrs

As has been noted so far, women have been making a significant difference in the church since the very beginning. It is clear from the beginning of Christianity that women have been followers of Christ and witnesses to the Resurrection. Even though they continued to be treated as second-class citizens and the weaker sex, that did not stop them from teaching, preaching, and living a gospel-centered life. Women were among the first martyrs of the church.[69]

From the earliest time, even before Saul's conversion, he "made havoc of the church, entering into every house and arresting men and women, committing them to prison" (Acts 8:3). Not satisfied with persecuting Christians in Jerusalem, Saul "yet breathing out threatenings and slaughter against the disciples of the Lord, went to the high priest and asked him for letters to the synagogues in Damascus that if he found any of them, whether men or women, he might bring them bound to Jerusalem" (Acts 9:1–2). These women could have protected themselves by keeping quiet, but they did not. Nor did their daughters in the faith later refrain from proclaiming Christ in the act of torture and death. Rather, they led the vanguard, lighting the way for others.

The earliest secular accounts of Christians who suffered for their faith bears witness to three women. We find written in Annales Xiii32, AD 57 the trial of Pomponia Graecina, a woman of high rank, who was accused of "foreign superstition" and handed over to her husband as judge for trial. This woman was the first Christian persecuted for the faith that history records outside the New Testament. She suffered for her testimony even before the New Testament was completed.[70]

Pliny the Younger writes in his letter to Trajan (AD 112) about applying torture to two maidservants, who were probably slaves, and were quite young. Yet they were recognized publicly as Christian ministers. Their witness for Christ must have been public, for they were arrested and tortured to incriminate the rest of the church.[71]

The apostle Peter's wife was martyred before Peter was. This was during the Neronian persecution at Rome. But it was Blandina who was confessed by the Gentiles as the one martyr who suffered more than any other martyr. She was recognized by the group of Christians as their greatest martyr. She not only endured more than all the others, but she continually encouraged and prayed for them. As a spiritual mother, she strengthened them to remain steadfast for Christ by her exhortations and example. Blandina's example was a witness to the persecutors and the crowds of her leadership and faith in Christ.[72]

M. Women as Missionaries

Not only were women among the first martyrs, but they were also among the first missionaries.

Unofficial writings indicate that the wives of the apostles assisted in missionary work, and this was one of the ways that the gospel reached the women's quarters of households.

Thecla (first century) was visited by Paul and Barnabas on their first missionary journey. She was a native of Iconium in Asia Minor and became a Christian. Details of her life are obscure, but she is mentioned in the writings of Augustine and other church fathers. Two churches were dedicated to her, and some believe she may have founded a convent near Seleucia. There is some indication that she was the first martyr in Greece. It is known that she taught the teachings of Paul and was a devout Christian of her day.[73]

The most successful woman missionary of the ancient church was Nino, "the apostle of Georgia." She was a slave from Cappadocia whose miraculous healing abilities brought her to the attention of the queen of Georgia. Nino healed her in the name of Christ. Eventually the king was converted and built a church. Nino's influence brought about the conversion of the country of Georgia to Orthodox Christianity from the top down.[74]

One can see from this wide survey of data that women played powerful, pervasive, and precious roles in the life of the early church. From their fortitude and beauty in the face of horrible martyrdom, to their power and thoroughness in scholarship and teaching, they honored the Lord. They served the church. They fed the church. They truly played their part in proclaiming the gospel to all nations.[75]

N. Story and Questions to Ponder

In many Catholic colleges, before the Vatican Council II church, women were not allowed to take any theology or canon law courses. There were some understanding professors who allowed women to sit outside the classroom and listen and take notes. In that situation, the professor would leave his door open so they could listen in on his lectures and hear what was being said in class. Of course, it was different on the campus of one university. One elderly sister recalled that women were also not allowed to take theology classes there—but religious nuns were, because they were not considered women.

1. If you were one of the nuns who was allowed into the theology class, how would you feel?

2. What do you think was the reason given for women not being allowed to take theology classes?

3. In the Calendar of the Saints—saints were considered spiritual guides. Who is or who has been your spiritual guides?

C H A P T E R   8

Leadership in the Church

A. All Called to Leadership

When looking at the leadership in the church, a good place to begin is by looking at Jesus. What was Jesus's mission? Was it to start his own church? I don't think so. Jesus did not create any formal church structure. He pointed his followers toward a new vision that did not include the notion of a concrete religious structure or church. In fact, the word *church* only occurs in one gospel, the gospel of Matthew.[76] The gospel writers chose to use the word *kingdom*, not church. It appears that Jesus never meant to start a new religion or church. Instead he wanted to help people see beyond their earthly divisions and distinctions toward a new, broader kingdom of God's justice, toward a realm where all are called to serve and minister. So—as we look at the early growth of leadership and ministry, what we do find is ministry done in the spirit of Christ without distinction between who is eligible to minister, because all the believers were eligible.

> For all of you who were baptized into Christ have clothed yourselves with Christ. There is neither Jew nor Greek, there is neither slave nor free man, there is neither male nor female; for you are all one in Christ Jesus. And if you belong to Christ, then

you are Abraham's descendants, heirs according to promise. (Galatians 3:25–29)

It is in this same spirit that early ministry was conceived, with no disciplinary or authority structure. All people had gifts of the spirit, and all people, men and women together, were called to use these gifts in ministry to their community.

In the days of St. Paul, the people who used their gifts were given various titles. The most common titles were:

- prophet
- teacher
- apostle/disciples

The apostles and disciples were eyewitnesses to the resurrection and were commissioned by the resurrected Lord to missionary work, and according to all four gospels, women fulfilled this criteria as well as men.

B. First-Century Didache to the Council of Trent

It was during the first century that the church begins to put into documentary form the church's legal system. The first century introduced us to the first church document that attempted to put together in one script the rules concerning baptism, Eucharist, the organization of the Christian community, and the selection and consecration of church officials.

Starting in the second century, there is an increasing use of the words *deacon, presbyter,* and *episkopos* that later became associated with the titles we know today as deacon, priest, and bishop. It was also in the second century that we begin to have evidence of an ordination ritual. The document, *The Apostolic Tradition of Hippolytus of Rome,* brings us the oldest known ordination ritual for episkopos, presbyter, and deacon. This text, which was written in the year 218, contained rules concerning the consecration of bishops, priests, and deacons, as well as regulations for confessors, catechumens, lectors, and other rules and directives concerning life in the community of believers.

What were the requirements for episkopos in the second century? They were: someone who had pastoral, liturgical and/or administrative functions; someone with moral character, teaching, and preaching abilities; and fifty years old, the husband of only one wife.

The document reads,

> Let the episkopos be ordained after he has been chosen by all the people. When he has been named and shall please all, let him, with the presbytery and such bishops as may be present, assemble with the people on a Sunday. While all give their consent, the bishops shall lay their hands upon him.[77]

What becomes clear is that this document helps us to see that ordination was not something that has been with us since the time of Jesus, but that ordination evolved as ministry became increasingly restricted to men and a liturgical focus rather than encompassing the early service- leadership model that was shared by most Christians.

The word *ordination* developed from the Roman usage of the words *ordo* or *ordines*, which referred to the hierarchical order of people in Rome who were eligible for leadership positions in government. Therefore, when clerical leaders used the word *ordination*, they were aware that the word contained exclusive connotations. Similarly, the clergy chose Greco-Roman terminology that separated men in ordained office from others by using the word *laity* and *clergy*.

The word *laity* comes from the word *laikoi*, which referred to those in Greco-Roman society who were not educated or ordained and had no order within the established political structure. Therefore, when formal church leaders began to use the terminology "laypeople" within the church, this language had the effect of setting up two classes of people—the educated and the uneducated, or another way of saying this would be the ordained and the laity. Laypeople were, then, essentially not ordered or part of church structure.[78]

In the third century, there developed local councils, which began to issue local laws or canons for different local and national regions. The first council that took place was the Council of Nicaea. This council was the first ecumenical council of the church—ecumenical meaning worldwide. This was the first of its kind, in the sense that it was not just a local or regional council, but it was universal, encompassing all the known world, which, at that time, was the Roman Empire. Most significantly, it resulted in the first uniform Christian doctrine, called the Nicene Creed.[79] With the creation of the creed, a precedent was established for subsequent local and regional councils of bishops to create statements of belief—the intent being to define unity of beliefs for the whole of Christendom.

C. Female Deacons

At this time there is also evidence of a special ordained office for female deacons, or deaconesses, and also an order of widows that had developed in the Eastern Christian communities. However, it must be noted that evidence of deaconesses at this time was not always a positive sign. Deaconesses became a reminder that the church was slowly edging women out of recognized ministry and relegating them to lower levels of office according to what was understood to be their inferior spiritual status and polluting sexuality.

In the fourth century the document *The Apostolic Constitution* added the office of virgins in church structure. No longer are all women exercising leadership functions but only those who, as virgins and widows, transcended sex roles.[80]

The early church councils continued to address the question of female deacons. The Council of Nicaea, in the early part of the fourth century, did not consider deaconesses as part of the clergy. However, by the time of the Council of Chalcedon in 451, they were clearly counted among the clergy.[81]

In the year 451, the Council of Chalcedon declared that a woman must be over forty years of age in order to be ordained a deacon, prompting some scholars to believe that this was created so as to keep menstruating women out of formal ministry.[82]

The Second Council of Orleans in 533 acknowledged the existence of female deacons but wanted to put a stop to the practice.[83] There was an order of widows and virgins—but then some wives of wealthy kings and landowners wanted a special blessing of ordination, and they were called deaconesses. At that time the word *deaconesses* became the terms used for the wives of deacons. But the council wanted to put a stop to this practice as well. Many different reasons were given for this, some reasons based on the assumption that women were inferior beings and objects of and temptations to sin. Apparently, it was okay to form the order of widows and virgins, because they were seen as not approachable sexually.

During the eleventh and twelfth centuries, although the presence of women in formally recognized ministry had declined over the centuries, there was evidence of a pope confirming the practice of ordaining women deacons in a letter written to a Portuguese bishop in the eleventh century. Pope Benedict VIII writes to the Bishop of Porto in 1017, "We concede and confirm to you and to your successors in perpetuity every Episcopal ordination, not only of presbyters but also of deacons and deaconesses or sub-deacons."[84] The evidence is clear that women were ordained as deacons. This can be found in early church documents such as the *Didascalia Apostolorum*. According to the baptismal ritual described in the *Didascalia*, after the celebrant anointed only the head of a woman to be baptized, the deaconess would apply the holy oil over the whole body. The deaconess acted as the godmother and would be responsible for instructing her in the faith. At that time, social custom prohibited a bishop from sending a deacon to minister to Christian women in a pagan household. So, the bishop would assign a deaconess to visit these women and fulfill their various needs, including catechesis, nursing care, or whatever pastoral care was needed.[85]

Later, found in the *Apostolic Constitutions,* this document portrays deaconesses as a definite order open only to virgins or widows of proven character who received the rite of ordination. Like other clerics, deaconesses were to be ordained within the sanctuary by the imposition of hands and the prayer of the bishop celebrated in the presence of the priests, the deacons, and the deaconesses.[86]

The Barberini Greek pontifical, most likely from southern Italy, familiar in the Eastern Church from the fourth to the twelfth century, contained a rite for the ordination of deaconesses. This rite was used in the Byzantine ordo, and it attempted to structure a ritual as parallel as possible to that of the deacons. The deaconess was always ordained at the foot of the altar in the sanctuary, the same place where a deacon was ordained. There were other similarities in the deacon and deaconess ordinations. The bishop would pray with his hands on the head of the deaconess to be ordained. He would pray that she be given the gift of the diaconate in the Holy Spirit, just as Phoebe was. Then the bishop would place the stole around her neck. After she received Eucharist, the bishop would then give the chalice to the deaconess, who would take it and put it on the altar. According to some scholars, these ordination formulas and ceremonies demonstrate that this was not just a blessing, but it was a matter of ordination on a par with the ordination of a deacon, and ordination in the strictest sense whose formally sacramental character cannot be questioned. Having received a "sacred ordination," the deaconess was clearly considered part of the clergy in official canonical terms. [87]

After the institution of deacons and of deaconesses spread and flourished in various local churches for several centuries, cultural and ecclesial changes exerted profound effects on these offices and eventually led to their decline. Culture played a major role in the changes and roles of deacons in the following centuries.

The evidence is clear: women have always done ministry, but recognition of this ministry became suppressed through the centuries. As women's ministry becomes less visible in our church's history, men's ministry becomes more prominent.

It is from this time in history that the priesthood and ministry became increasingly cultic and Eucharist-focused, rather than service-oriented. It is believed that this Eucharistic-centered focus had its roots in the structuring of church ministry, and once this practice was theologized by the scholastic theologians, it became the main approach to priestly practice and theology for about seven hundred years.

As the role of deacon took on a more structured role and less a service-oriented role, deacons were then performing fewer functions. With deacons performing fewer functions, then the opportunity for deaconesses to function became more restricted and then totally disappeared.

During the course of these seven hundred years, the number of sacraments is set at seven for men and six for women.

During the Middle Ages, there were many movements of people who claimed the priesthood of all believers and tried to live a more inclusive, service-oriented ministry. It was at this time that a Benedictine monk, Gratian, put together what has been called *Gratian's Decretum*. This was a collection of nearly thirty-eight hundred texts touching on all areas of church discipline and regulation. It soon became the basic text on which the masters of canon law lectured and commented on in the universities.[88]

The work was not just a collection of texts but also a treatise attempting to resolve the apparent contradictions and discordances in the rules accumulated from different sources. When necessary, Gratian had recourse to the Roman law and made extensive use of the works of the church fathers and of ecclesiastical writers.

For centuries the *Decretum* was the text on which the teaching of canon law in the schools was based. It became the first part of the *Corpus Juris Canonici*, the great body of canon law, and it served as an important source for the official codification of canon law in 1917 and its revision in 1983. It soon became the basic text on which the masters of canon law lectured and commented on in the universities.[89]

The presumed inferiority of women entered church law especially through *Gratian's Decretals*. This became the official church law in 1234 and a vital part of the canon law of the church that was in force until 1916. These modes of conduct and ways of thinking were expressed in the *Decretals*.

- Women signified weakness of mind.
- In everything a wife is subject to her husband because of her state of servitude.
- Women are not created in the image of God.
- Wives are subject to their husbands by nature.
- Women may not be given a liturgical office in the church.
- Women cannot become priests or deacons.
- Women may not teach in church.
- Women may not teach or baptize.

This teaching is found in the *Corpus Iuris Canonici*:[90]

- "By a principle of civil law, no woman can exercise a public office. By church law, women are equally barred from all spiritual functions and office."
- "A woman can, therefore, not receive any ecclesiastical ordination. If she receives one, the ordination will not imprint a sacramental character ..."
- "No women, however saintly she may be, may neither preach nor teach."
- "A wife is under the power of her husband, the husband, not under the power of the wife. The husband may punish her. A wife is obliged to follow her husband to wherever he decides to fix his residence."
- "A woman is bound to greater modesty than a man."

- "A woman is sooner excused on account of fear than a man. She is dispensed from going to Rome to obtain absolution from an excommunication."

The Council of Trent was called in 1545–63. This council reconfirmed a theology of male priesthood and emphasized a priesthood based on the Eucharist as sacrifice rather than ministerial service. During the council, there was no mention of preaching the word, no mention of leading the community in service. The view on priesthood and the sacrament of ordination remained relatively similar from the Council of Trent to the late nineteenth and early twentieth centuries.

In the year 1917, Pope Pius X attempted to codify the canonical tradition into a coherent whole. The actual work was done by a commission of Cardinals headed by Cardinal Pietro Gasparri. After consultation with the bishops and major superiors throughout the world, the code was promulgated by Pope Benedict XV on May 27, 1917.

Before concluding this section regarding women deacons, it is important to note that, in 1995 the Canon Law Society of America published a report concerning "The Canonical Implications of Ordaining Women to the Permanent Diaconate." They reached the following conclusions:

- Historically, women have been ordained as deaconesses.

- The supreme authority of the church is competent to decide to ordain women to the permanent diaconate. This would require a derogation from canon 1024, which restricts all ordinations to males. However, this can be done by legislation or individual indults to episcopal conferences.

- The ordination to the diaconate for women would not necessarily have to be adopted throughout the entire church. This can be a question that is left to decisions by the episcopal conference and individual diocesan bishops.

In summary, canonically, a decision to ordain women to the permanent diaconate is possible. Appropriate procedures would have to be followed. For example, sufficient reason would have to be given for the Apostolic See to grant an indult to the bishops of a country to derogate from canon 1024, which restricts ordination to the permanent diaconate to males, and to adjust the application of various canons dealing with irregularities and impediments, as well as with clerical obligations and rights, so that they would be phrased in terms applicable to women as well as to men.

In effect, the amount of adjustments in law that would be required to open the permanent diaconate to women are within the authority of the church to make and are relatively few in number. The practical effect, however, would be to open up ordained ministry as permanent deacons to women, enabling them to receive all seven sacraments, and making them capable of assuming offices that entail the exercise of the diaconal order and of ecclesiastical jurisdiction, which are now closed to women. [91]

D. The 1917 Code of Canon Law

Under the 1917 Code of Canon Law, although no canon explicitly defined the inferior legal status of women, numerous norms limited the participation of women in the teaching, sanctifying, and governing mission of the church. The church's negative view characterized women as:

- subordinate to man
- seductive and an occasion of sin
- intellectually inferior and lacking judgment
- timid, scrupulous, and in need of protection

This kind of thinking continued where *Gratian's Decretals* left off. Several studies indicated that such discriminatory legislation had its foundation in several other sources as well: a too fundamental interpretation of sacred scripture, writings of church leaders taken out of context, critical adherence to Roman law, legislation aimed at protecting the celibate clergy, and the gradual clericalization and hierarchical ordering of church ministry.

Several canons in the 1917 Code presented a passive and inferior role for women in *liturgical functions.* For example:

- Canon 813.2: "The minister serving at Mass should not be a woman unless, in the absence of a man, for a just cause, it is so arranged that the woman respond from afar and by no means approach the altar."

- Canon 910.1: "The confessions of women should not be heard outside of a confessional seat except in cases of illness or other true necessity, and following the precautions that the local ordinary decides are opportune."

- Canon 910.2: "The confessions of men may be heard licitly even in any private building."

- Canon 1262.1: "It is desirable that, consistent with ancient discipline, women be separated from men in church."

- Canon 1262.2: "Men, in a church or outside a church, while they are assisting a sacred rites, shall be bare-headed, unless the approved norms of the people or peculiar circumstances of things determine otherwise; women, however, shall have a covered head and be modestly dressed, especially when they approach the table of the Lord."

Other canons reflect an understanding of a woman as *subordinate to her husband in marriage*. For example:

- Canon 1112: "Unless special law provides otherwise, the wife, as far as canonical effects are concerned, is made a sharer in the status of her husband."

- Canon 1223.2: "A wife and pubescent children are entirely immune in this selection from the power of the husband and parents."

Some canons implied that *women were sinful or dangerous* by prohibiting their physical proximity to men, particularly the celibate clergy. For example:

- Canon 133.1: "Clerics should take care not to retain or in other ways to frequent women upon whom suspicion can fall."

- Canon 133.3: "The judgment about retaining or frequenting women even those who commonly fall under no suspicion, in particular cases where scandal is possible or where there is given a danger of incontinence, belongs to the local Ordinary who can prohibit clerics from retaining or frequenting such women."

There are also the following canons based on a *woman's presumed inferiority*. For example:

- Canon 93.1: "A wife who is not legitimately separated from her husband, automatically retains her husband's domicile."

- Canon 118: "Only male clerics can hold the power of orders or ecclesiastical jurisdiction, or obtain benefices and ecclesiastical pensions."

- Canon 709: "With regard to confraternities or pious unions established to promote devotional or charitable work, women cannot be given membership in them, except for the purpose of gaining indulgences and spiritual graces granted to the male members."

- Canon 2004.1: "In the canonization process, anyone of the faithful can request that a case be instigated ... men can act through themselves or through a properly appointed procurator, women only through a procurator."

A summary of the message given by these canons is simple: theologians, as well as church canonists, accepted the inferiority of women. If it was accepted in Greek and Roman law, then it was accepted in church law. *The 1917 Code of Canon Law* enshrined the inferiority of women. It became a presumption that women were the inferior and weaker sex. There really was no question—it was just a given.

E. Women and the Right to Vote

At the same time that women were subjected to such an inferior role in the church, there occurred two major breakthroughs for women in the United States. First, women were granted the right to vote.[92] On July 19, 1848, was the first gathering of women devoted to giving women this right. The principal organizers of the Seneca Falls Convention were Elizabeth Cady Stanton and Lucretia Mott. At that convention, Stanton drafted what was called a "Declaration of Sentiments, Grievances and Resolutions." One of the resolutions written in this declaration echoed the *Declaration of Independence*: "We hold these truths to be self-evident; that all men and women are created equal."

Stanton and Susan B. Anthony, a Massachusetts teacher, met in 1850 and forged a lifetime alliance as women's rights activists.

For much of the 1850s they agitated against the denial of basic economic freedoms to women. Later, they unsuccessfully lobbied Congress to include women in the provisions of the Fourteenth and Fifteenth Amendments (extending citizenship rights and granting voting rights to freedmen, respectively).

Late in the 1880s and 1890s the nation began to experience a surge of volunteerism among middle-class women—activists in progressive causes, members of women's clubs and professional societies, temperance advocates, and participants in local civic and charity organizations.

There was a suffragist parade in New York City in 1916. In that parade a banner flew with the words, *"President Wilson favors votes for women."* Woodrow Wilson, a reluctant convert to the cause, eventually supported the Nineteenth Amendment, which passed the house in 1918 and was ratified by the states in 1920.

The first state to grant women complete voting rights was Wyoming in 1869, followed by three other western states—Colorado (1893), Utah (1896), and Idaho (1896). But prior to 1910, only these four states allowed women to vote. By 1914 additional states extended the franchise to women: Washington, California, Arizona, Kansas, and Oregon.

When Woodrow Wilson decided to take a stand in World War I and used the phrase that we must make *"the world safe for democracy,"* women used that phrase to insist that democracy begins at home. Moreover, they insisted, the failure to extend the vote to women might impede their participation in the war effort just when they were most needed to play a greater role as workers and volunteers outside the home.

Responding to these overtures, the House of Representatives initially passed a voting rights amendment on January 10, 1918, but the Senate did not follow suit before the end of the sixty-fifth Congress. It was not until after the war, however, that the measure finally cleared Congress with the House again voting its approval by a wide margin on May 21, 1919, and the Senate concurring on

June 14, 1919. A year later, on August 26, 1920, the Nineteenth Amendment, providing full voting rights for women nationally, was ratified when Tennessee became the thirty-sixth state to approve it.

After the right to vote however, began the long, arduous task of securing women a measure of power in local and national political office.

F. The National Council of Catholic Women

The year 1920 was a very significant year for women. Not only was it a breakthrough for women in terms of voting rights, but it was also the year of the founding of the *National Council of Catholic Women (NCCW)*. Catholic laywomen had always been involved in charitable work. But when it came to fighting for the right to vote, many Catholic women remained aloof, partly because of their own conservative attitudes, but also because of widespread clerical disapproval of the vote for women.[93]

Cardinal James Gibbons, archbishop of Baltimore, was a strong opponent of women's rights. He feared that if women insisted on their rights to political participation, they would be "distracted from their true vocation which was the home and the cultivation of the domestic virtues of love of their husbands and children."[94]

However, just as the fervor of the suffragette movement was taking place, so was the fervor behind women's devotion to their church, and thus the beginning of the NCCW. The women wanted to bring together all of their local church groups into one organized society. They recognized that their goal of giving voice to millions of US Catholic women and "harnessing their efforts for the good of the church could best be accomplished within a single national federation under episcopal sponsorship."[95]

So—even though the *National Council of Catholic Women* took major steps in bringing women together to work in the church, it was only when the Vatican Council took place in 1963 that the church dared to claim that the church is not the hierarchy made up of male clergy, and the church is not "the perfect society." Instead, the church can be understood as "the people of God." This was a sign of a new beginning. But where did the women fit in?

G. Second Vatican Council

Then, a change began to take place—the *Council of Vatican II* was called by Pope John XXIII in 1959. A major shift took place at this council. The laity were no longer considered passive spectators, as was directed in Pope Pius X's encyclical *Vehementer Nos* of 1906 when it states the laity "have no other right than to let themselves be guided and so follow their pastors in docility."[96] Now, with the Vatican Council being called to order, there was a major shift in ecclesiology.

This major shift indicated that the laity share equally in being gifted with the Holy Spirit, being called to holiness and being engaged in the mission of the church. Pope Pius XII's statement that the "laity are the church" came as a startling revelation to most Catholics, and this became the heart of the documents from Vatican II—the church as the people of God was absolutely revolutionary.

The idea of a *Second Vatican Council* was in the minds of many before it was called to order. In the early decades of the century, the writings of Europe's leading thinkers, among them Karl Rahner, Hans Kung, and Yves Congar, had proposed a decisive shift toward a more open and outgoing Catholicism. Most of these progressives had been branded as dissidents by Rome because of their rock-boat teachings and had been silenced or disciplined at one time or another by Vatican superiors. It took the "goodwill and the boldness of Pope John XXIII to bring the dissidents in from the cold."[97]

The Vatican Council was the most monumental event of the twenty-first-century church. This council was going to attempt to address the widening gap between Catholicism and modernity. Up until this point in history, there was a movement toward separation of clergy and laity. The call to holiness was only possible through separation from the world—so there was no real purpose in dealing with the laity. They were just the subjects of the hierarchy—this view prevailed in the church right up until the council itself. Up until this time, there were two classes of people—clergy and lay—and lay had no role.

The council had a large impact on the future framework of women religious. Changes were affecting how women religious dressed, worked, and prayed. This council was attempting to address how the church could be more relevant to the world, and the pope was specifically addressing women religious. Pope John XXIII actually shocked the church by calling this council. Supposedly he was too old, and he was elected largely with the assumption that he would not serve long, but long enough to give the cardinals a chance to determine a longer-term candidate. He surprised them all.

There were twenty-three hundred world bishops, cardinals, and archbishops. A select number of non-Catholics were also invited as observers with limited speaking privileges. Wives of the representatives of other Christian churches were allowed into the sessions as observers. Officials from non-Christian religions were likewise invited, as were Catholic laymen. But no women were involved in the council. Their views, opinions, or comments were not solicited in any way. No Catholic women were invited. The council had an incredible effect on women's religious communities—the council was telling women religious that they had to modify their habits, and their way of living should be more conducive to the world in which they live. Yet—no religious were invited to the council to listen or to be listened to. It was only when the council was half over that one cardinal pled the women's cause—especially women religious whose lifestyle, dress, and apostolate were being questioned. Cardinal Suenens from Brussels reminded those at the council that Vatican II was not representing "half of humanity."[98] Rome's response was to invite twenty-three women to the third and fourth sessions as auditors. They gathered with the nearly three thousand men in attendance. There they were—watching and listening, but not allowed to speak. No wonder the nuns at the council wondered what the council had to do with them—they were an afterthought. The invitation had arrived late, and it had conditions attached.

One of the twenty-three invited women was Sister Mary Luke Tobin from the United States. She was, at that time, superior of the Sisters of Loretto and also president of the *Conference of Major Superiors of Women Religious.* She recalled later that, while at the council, she encountered Ildebrando Cardinal Antoniutti, head of the Vatican department in charge of religious orders. On one occasion, she was summoned by the cardinal after he saw a picture in the paper of one of her sisters in a newly modified habit. She remarked: "He never looked me straight in the eye." Instead, she said, "He took the picture, took a pen, and drew the skirt down, the sleeves down, then added a little veil."[99]

Sister Tobin also recalls that, on the last day of the council, there was an outdoor Mass to honor distinguished persons in various categories. First, four philosophers, followed by four literati, four musicians, and so on, were singled out for praise. Finally, four women walked across the stage. The announcer proclaimed that "women should be honored for their contribution to the church." Sister Mary Luke, at that point, turned to her nearest neighbor in the bleachers, Father Godfrey Diekmann, and said, "But women are not a *category* in the church. They should not be honored as women more than men should be honored as men. Men and women are the church, aren't they?"[100]

In Sister Carmel McEnroy's book *Guests in Their Own House,* she writes of the sisters' experience at the council. She stated that a few of the bishops approved their presence, but most acted indifferently to their presence, and some just plain "looked scared."[101] Sister Gladys Parentelli in her book *Mujer Iglesia Liberacion* tells her readers that Archbishop Pericle Felici, who occupied the post of secretary of the council, never acknowledged the women or looked in their direction, even though he sat close to where they were sitting. [102]

Barbara Ward, who was a British economist, was asked to prepare a paper on poverty and hunger, only to be barred from delivering it at a council session. Instead, a layman was called upon to read the paper.

There was one piece of good news however. A commission was formed and in charge of the Pastoral Constitution on the Church in the Modern World *Gaudium et Spes*. This commission asked six women auditors to attend their business session. The document on which they were able to cast their vote became one of the landmarks of the council promoting human rights and social justice. It was also one of the longest documents produced at the Council. Sister Luke Tobin can recite some of its passages from memory—even as she entered into her late eighties: "With respect to the fundamental rights of the person, every type of discrimination, whether social or cultural, whether based on sex, race, color, social condition, language or religion is to be overcome and eradicated as contrary to God's intent."[103]

Pope John XXIII opened the council on October 11, 1962, and Pope Paul VI closed the council on December 8, 1965. The Catholic Church, which was considered "the perfect society" before the council was now considered "the People of God." This was an absolutely dramatic turn of events. The words of the council made a beginning step toward knocking down the barriers between clergy and lay. Now the layperson was encouraged to take part in the Mass. The layperson was considered the church when the church became defined as "the people of God." The Mass celebrant now could face the people when celebrating and the Mass could be in the language of the people. Another major development from Vatican Council II was the fundamental equality of the baptized, and the universal call to holiness.[104] Of course, some Catholics continued to resist the changes, and others believed that the Council did not go far enough. This tension still exists in the church. The collision course between those who welcome and those who resist the changes still continue today.

H. The 1983 Code of Canon Law

The work of reforming and recodifying *the 1917 Code of Canon Law* was announced in 1959, but it had to await action until after the council was completed in 1965. Finally the New Code of Canon Law was promulgated in 1983 by the Apostolic Constitution *Sacrae disciplinae leges*. In this constitution, Pope John Paul added a new stress, which was developed as a result of the Vatican Council—that was the concept of church as the people of God.

Many of the canons with regard to discrimination between men and women were eliminated from the *1983 Code of Canon Law*. In this code there is more a distinction between the rights of the clergy versus the rights of the laity.

Canon 204 in the 1983 code makes it clear that all are called and all are sharers in Christ's priestly, prophetic, and royal office because of baptism. Canon 204 states,

> The Christian faithful are those who inasmuch as they have been incorporated in Christ through baptism are constituted as the people of God. For this reason, since they have become sharers in Christ's priestly, prophetic and royal office in their own manner, they are called to exercise the mission in which God has entrusted to the church to fulfill in the world in accord with the condition proper to each one.

Here it states that the sacrament of baptism is the sacrament of empowerment. From a canonical point of view, the sacrament of baptism gives all the same standing in the law. All are equal. There is not a male baptism and a female baptism. There is not a baptism for lay and a baptism for clergy. All the baptized are incorporated in Christ in the same way. And in that sense, there is a true equality in the law for both male and female. All share in Christ's priestly, prophetic, and royal office. And it is for precisely this reason that all are called to exercise the mission that God has entrusted the church. All are the leaven and the dough. All are the light on the hill. All are the salt that does not lose its flavor. In a real sense, it establishes the basis for the exercise of Christian leadership by all the faithful, and all the baptized share in the teaching, sanctifying, and governing mission in the church, which flows directly from this office of Christ.

This call to all of the baptized, whether men or women, is also found in the canons on the teaching office of the church. Canon 211 states,

> All the Christian faithful have the duty and the right to work so that the divine message of salvation may increasingly reach the whole of human kind in every age and in every land.

Another canon that impacts the teaching office of the church is canon 225.

> Since the laity are designated by God for the Apostolate through baptism and confirmation, they are bound by the general obligation and possess the rights as individuals, or joined in associations to work so that the divine message of salvation is made known and accepted by all persons everywhere in the world. This obligation is even more compelling in those circumstances in which only through them can people hear the gospel and know Christ.

These canons stress the obligation of the laity—again making no distinction between men or women, to work so that the divine message of salvation is made known. It is not an invitation but an obligation.

Another significant canon that bears notice in the teaching canons of the code is Canon 766: "Lay persons can be admitted to preach in a church or oratory if it is necessary in certain circumstances or if it is useful in particular cases."

This canon provides a broad possibility for lay preaching, a contrast to the 1917 code, which prohibited lay preaching. This openness to lay preaching was introduced in *Lumen Gentium*, where it states that all of the baptized must concern themselves with the proclamation of the gospel.[105]

One canon that does indicate a distinction between men and women is found in canon 230.

> Lay men who possess the age and qualification
> determined by decree of the conference of bishops
> can be *installed* on a stable basis in the ministries
> of lector and acolyte in accord with the prescribed
> liturgical right.

Of course we all know that both lay men and lay women serve as lectors in our church. The key word in this canon is the word *installed*. It specifically states that only lay men possess the qualifications to be installed. In section II of this canon it states, "Lay persons can fulfill the function of lector during liturgical actions by temporary deputation."

Section one of this canon speaks exclusively of installed ministers, and section two speaks of non-installed ministers. Section one refers to men, and section two refers to men and women. This is one of the rare canons that makes a distinction between men versus women.

When examining the canons related to the governing office in the church, the code makes it very clear who has the power of governance in the church, when it states, "In accord with the prescription of law those who have received the sacred orders are capable of the power of governance which exists in the church by divine institution and is also called the power of jurisdiction." This canon is canon 129 of the 1983 code.

It is quite clear from the reading of this canon that only those who are ordained are "capable" of possessing the power of governance in the church. The second part of the canon makes clear that lay people can "cooperate" in the power of governance but unclear as to what that means.

There are several offices open to laity that do imply the power of governance, and these positions are open to both men and women.

- Finance officer of a diocese—canon 494
- Finance officer of a religious institute—canon 636
- Member of a diocesan finance council—canon 492
- Lay person in charge of a parish—canon 517.2 (with certain conditions, however, basically when there is a shortage of priests)
- Administrator of ecclesiastical goods—canon 1279
- Judge—canon 1421.2 (however, only a cleric can serve in a single court tribunal)
- Auditor—canon 1428
- Promoter of justice—canon 1435
- Defender of the bond—canon 1435

More than ever, women are assuming church positions of authority and leadership. Women are found working in parishes, schools, and church administration. They serve on parish councils, work in parish offices, teach religious education, and are pastoral associates. They serve as canon lawyers, judges, and chancellors across the country. And as stated above, listing the proper canons, they serve as finance officers of a diocese (canon 494), can serve in charge of a parish if there is a shortage of priests (canon 517.2), and can serve as judges (canon 1421) as well as promoters of justice and defenders of the bond (canon 1435). They can be appointed chancellors (canon 482).

Perhaps most Catholics would not be surprised to learn that women make up about 83 percent of those in parish ministry, and many of them hold high-level administrative church positions in dioceses, social service agencies, and faith-based organizations.

Many of these women working in high-level administrative positions also hold unprecedented access to decision-making power. However, when the LCWR (Leadership Conference of Women Religious) completed a study on the experience of women in Catholic church administrative roles, the conclusion was a note of caution. The number of women holding high-level administration positions is increasing—yet it is still the exception rather than the norm. And, in the end, it is "by-and-large the ordained clergy who have the final say in major administrative decisions."[106]

At the same time that we can see the 1983 Code of Canon Law bringing new possibilities for a place for women in the church, it is still very clear as well that many roles in the church are reserved only for those in sacred orders. It is also very clear that "only a baptized male validly receives Sacred Ordination" (canon 1024). So, of course, women can still make the coffee, but can't make the decisions, since so much of the decision-making in the church is reserved for the ordained.

I. Leadership Equals Ordination

The traditional reasons for excluding women from ordination are varied. The following are arguments given for excluding women from the priesthood:

1. The Sacred—Sacramental Argument

From the beginning of the third century onward, as we have seen in this brief study, the person of the minister and his liturgical actions came to be regarded as sacred. Since sexuality was thought to be unclean and improper in this sacred sphere, "the priest had to be unmarried and women were excluded from sacred functions because of their periodic uncleanness." Also, the Christian priesthood is therefore of a sacramental nature, the priest is a sign, which the faithful must be able to recognize with ease. St. Thomas says, "Sacramental signs represent what they signify by natural resemblance." This same natural resemblance is required for persons as for things: when Christ's role in the Eucharist is to be expressed sacramentally, there would not be this "natural resemblance," which must exist between Christ and his minister if the role of Christ were not taken by a man; in such a case it would be difficult to see in the minister the image of Christ, for Christ himself was and remains a man.[107]

2. The Philosophical Argument

In St. Augustine's influence—"man" is created in the image of God with power and reasoning—he also asserted the inferiority of the female sex to the male sex. The rationale for the exclusion of women in the official ministry of the church is closely linked to women's "natural" incapacity."[108]

3. The Subordination Argument

St. Thomas Aquinas presumes the biological inferiority of women. Under the headings of impediments to orders, the first article deals with the impediment of the female sex. Aquinas argues that a woman cannot be a priest because she has a subordinate status, and because of this subordinate status, a woman is incapable of rising through the various orders or hierarchy. [109]

4. The Sociological Argument

The exclusion of women from the priesthood is linked by some to the beginnings of the Christian church when the general status of women in society was inferior. Some degree of anti-feminism, which one often finds in the fathers of the church and authors of the Middle Ages, may have been derived from a somewhat contemptuous attitude toward women, sociologically and culturally speaking. Such attitudes certainly had the effect, at certain periods, of putting restrictions upon even the legitimate ministries of women.[110]

5. The Tradition Argument

Early church fathers call it a heretical error to admit women to the office and dignity of the priesthood. Basically, this argument stated that, since its beginning the church has not ordained women, and it's certainly not time now to change.[111]

6. The Ecclesiastical Law Argument

Some in the church believe that the exclusion of women from orders is of divine law and can never be changed, and others feel that the exclusion is of ecclesiastical law and change is possible. One author who seems to uphold the ecclesiastical law argument is Raoul Nax in a commentary on canon 968. He claims that both the order of widows and the order of deaconesses occupied a place in the ecclesiastical hierarchy. Granting that women did receive even one of the sacramental orders at some time in the history of the church, it follows, to Nax, that the exclusion from the sacrament of orders is an ecclesiastical, not a divine law.[112]

7. The Hierarchic Argument

Yves Congar has reassessed some of his earlier opinions as expressed in his book *Lay People in the church*. Still, his thinking on the hierarchical order of creation is still around. In this concept Congar sees the economy of God on earth as patterned on the same hierarchical structure as "the eternal mystery of God." He applied the same principle to the man-woman relationship: "We are told in Genesis that man was made in God's image. The woman is made in the image of the man, for she is derived from him, dependent on him, and so to say, his 'opposite number,' his fellow creature and his partner ..." and he sees in this relationship the law of divine economy "whereby a principle of help and fulfillment is joined to a principle of authority or hierarchy."[113]

8. In *Persona Christi*

Many trace it back to "in persona Christi," which states that a priest has to be the model of Christ, and it carries with this the understanding of gender. It rests on what is understood as Christian anthropology.

In conclusion, one can see that all of the above arguments are basically a repetition of the same argument. The church does not allow for equality, and women are still considered inferior.

J. Story and Questions to Ponder

Mary had been working as director of religious education for two years when the pastor announced that a new pastoral center would be built for the parish. This center would accommodate offices for the parish staff as well as a conference center for parish functions and parish meetings. Mary was asked to meet with the facilities manager.

The manager wanted to set up a meeting with her to go over the plans for her new office. She sat down with him, and he showed her the blueprint of the new building. In the plan he showed her, she was given a spacious office with a window and a seating area where she would hold meetings, or meet with parents. It was so much larger than what she presently had, and Mary was more than delighted. When an open house was planned to show off the new building, Mary discovered her office was a tiny cubicle at the end of the hall. When she went to confront the manager as to what happened with the beautiful office outlined in the blueprint, the manager told her that there were two sets of blueprints—one was the real set, and the second set existed solely to "keep her quiet." He told her that he had the fake blueprints ready to show her instead of the real blueprints because he could not stand to "watch her fuss" about the small size of her new office.

1. Have you ever had an experience similar to Mary's experience—afraid to be told the truth because of someone's presumption of how you would respond?

2. Can you think of a time in your ministry when you were consulted and your voice was heard, and it made a difference in a major decision—and the opposite?

3. The 1983 Code of Canon Law has certainly made it possible for lay leadership in the church. Have you witnessed any new positions that have been recently open to women in your parish or diocese?

CHAPTER 9

Conclusion

The Women Were Not Invited—but They Showed Up Anyway

In the late 1950's, before Betty Freidan wrote her famous and landmark book *The Feminine Mystique,* it was pretty clear the role of women in society. Their role was pretty much expressed in the fairy tales that were told at that time in our culture. The typical fairy tales—whether it be *The Ugly Duckling* or the *Little Engine that Could*—spoke volumes of what women's roles were. Remember the tale of the *Sleeping Beauty?* At one time this was the most often repeated fairy tale in Western culture. In general, the story includes the birth of a beautiful female, a fairy godmother, a revengeful curse, a sleep of one hundred years. Then enter the handsome prince destined to save the sleeping beauty and her people, and the kiss that awakens the sleeping beauty, who is now saved by the charming prince, and they live happily ever after. This image of the sleeping beauty has often, in the past, described how society defined the role of women. Society told us that, for women, her role was to be beautiful and docile and only fulfilled when she meets the man who will finally bring her life into significance. The moral of the fairy tale could easily be "a helpless woman need only wait patiently for a great strong man to rescue her."

During the time of our mothers and/or our grandmothers, the role of women was to be sweet, caring, quiet, dependent, and weak. Our culture in the past did all it could do to enhance this role, this image of women. Even growing up, it was the girl who was given the dolls and was told not to play rough; that was all right for boys but very unladylike. When the girl skinned her knee or bumped her head, she enjoyed more soothing, protective assurances. Why? Because she belonged to the weaker sex. She was expected to be cleaner than little boys, and certainly more manageable. In our culture, peer pressure also continued to inhibit this little girl, discouraging her from being too assertive or too individualistic. She learned the art of fading into the background. Such things as competition, individualism, seen as virtues for men, were frowned on and discouraged as unfeminine for women. Girls, as they grew up in the past, were taught to fulfill two roles. One—she is to be the desirable object, schooled in the art of passivity, and good only for her looks. Her second role was to live for another. This role would school her in self-forgetfulness, service, and sacrifice, in nurturing rather than initiating behavior. This role would teach her to be like the sleeping beauty, who learned how to wait, forever, if necessary, for the expected charming prince who would make her life meaningful and fulfilled.

We have by now discovered what is wrong with this image of women in the past. This sleeping beauty image for women that was so prevalent in our society undermined any idea that a woman might possibly be man's equal and entitle her to a self-fulfilling relationship. Women, men, and society have made great strides, as we all know. The economy of the country had a lot to do with changing the image of women since they had to work full time to make enough money for their family. A family could not often just depend on the finances made by the man of the household.

We live in a world where everything seems up for grabs. On the one hand, there is nothing wrong with being a housewife staying home and baking cookies and standing by her man. Yet, on the other hand there is also nothing wrong with striving and fighting for the right to be, not only first lady but president, and not only working in the church alongside a priest, but striving to be priest or bishop. What society tells us women's role is one thing, but the myth of women's weakness has also played havoc in the church and in our spiritual life as well. This can even be more devastating in many ways, because this touches the core of what it is to be human and made in the image of God.

Women in the Catholic church are so used to being treated poorly that many of them honestly believe they really are inferior to men. And of course, it is difficult to change a mind-set that was a form of belief and practice since the early beginnings of the church. Women have been taught from infancy that God is male-like and therefore males are God-like. Women have related to God rather exclusively through men by whom they were baptized and confirmed, who presided over their marriage or their religious vows, and who would anoint them at the hour of death. The word of God was preached to women by men, and as women, they were excluded from the study of theology, which would give women independent access to study the word. Marriage problems, vocational crisis, and the religious doubts of women were all handled by men. Even a religious congregation composed entirely of women could not open or close a chapter, elect a superior, amend its constitutions, or receive the vows of its new members without the presence of a man. Our theology and our law have also been dominated by male interpretation. Church law has been written by men, legislated by men, and interpreted by men. It is only recently that female theologians have risen up and are offering new perspectives in theological insights. Governance in the church, (expressed clearly in canon 129 and 1024) makes it clear that many church positions are only offered and allowed the ordained.

It is the gifts of many in the church that are being denied and pushed aside because of gender. A lot has changed in the church— but many have heard the expression that the more things change, the more things remain the same. That saying may be very true when it comes to the church. The church can and perhaps will continue to treat women as the inferior and weaker sex, but women have a name and a voice.

Hopefully this study has helped the reader to expand and deepen awareness of the consistent and historical pattern of neglect and prejudice that the church holds against women. This prejudice is obvious in the church's patriarchal pattern of thinking since the time of Plato, Aristotle, and Thomas Aquinas. It has continued in the years where dogma and doctrine have instilled the belief that there is only one word to describe God, and that word is our "Father." It is also clear when examining the neglected stories of women in the Old Testament and at the time of Jesus that women, who were defined by patriarchy, were actually brave, courageous women, even prophets and judges. Jesus listened and paid attention to them. But when it comes to the lectionary, many of the readings recounting their bravery have been left out. Also, in examining the laws of the church, one sees very clearly that the pattern of prejudice that has existed from the beginning of the church's foundation is still alive and well. Yet even though women continued to go unnamed and unnoticed in the Old and New Testament, they were also teachers, followers, disciples, and deacons. They were not afraid to speak up and were filled with bravery. Yet a pattern that began a long time ago—that is the pattern of being unnamed and unnoticed—continues. The women were not invited—but guess what? They showed up anyway. At the beginning of this study, it was stated that women fill our churches and schools, our universities and soup kitchens, work at homeless shelters and administrative church positions. They serve as lectors, extraordinary ministers of communion, parish council officers, teachers, parish administrators, and canon lawyers. The list is endless. But somehow, they didn't get invited, and it's about time they were invited into full participation. But if that doesn't happen, our task is to make sure women will continue to show up despite the noninvitation. In summary, the message women are invited to take with them can be summarized with these important instructions.

1. Don't allow the institutional church to measure your worth. Jesus has already done this.

In studying and tracing the history of the institutional church's treatment of women, it is anything but exemplary. Allow Jesus to lead the way. Jesus is the one who, all along, paid attention to the women and called on them to be disciples. In the culture of that time, women were invisible and powerless to nearly everyone but Jesus. Allow Jesus to measure your worth, not the institutional church.

2. Your opinion matters.

We have heard of the television program *Father Knows Best*. Well—sometimes he does and sometimes he doesn't, and if he does know best, it's not because "priests are always right." Priests are human too, so let's not put them in a position of perfection. Their job is tough enough. But they need to hear from you. Offer your opinion to Father, and speak up when you have an opinion that needs to be heard. The faithful may disagree with their pastor in a particular situation over a specific issue. Women's role is to speak up if it is an issue that affects the common good of the church. Canon 212.2 and 212.3 states,

> The Christian faithful are free to make known to the pastors of the church their needs especially spiritual ones, and their desires. According to the knowledge, competence, and prestige, which they possess, they have the right and even at times the duty to manifest to the sacred pastors their opinion on matters which pertain to the good of the church and to make their opinion known to the rest of the Christian faithful, without prejudice to the integrity of faith and morals, with reverence toward their

pastors, and attentive to common advantage and the dignity of persons.

3. *Be a reminder to others that our God cannot be limited to only one image or one metaphor.*

We cannot box God into one image or metaphor. God is our Father, that's true. But the problem comes when only the word *Father* is used to describe God. Let's remind ourselves and others to multiply one's metaphors for God. If we are planning prayer services or teaching religion classes or leading a church group or committee, use different metaphors in addressing God. God is Father but also Mother. At the same time, God is she and he and neither. God is so much more. God is Helper, Comforter, Rock, Fountain, and Spring of Water. In that way, we can acknowledge that God is beyond anything we may imagine.

4. *Pay attention to what the women in the scriptures teach us.*

Remember, as the introduction to this book reminds us, Jesus recognized women for the gifts and the talents they bring to the world of hunger and need. Women do have a voice in the response they give, and they set the example for all those who care about the church. Our call is to pay attention and listen to what the women in the scriptures teach us.

- *Remember Deborah?* She can teach us strength and courage.
- *Remember Huldah?* She can teach us to speak the truth—a truth that sometimes is hard to hear but needs to be said.
- *Remember Miriam?* "Sing to the Lord, for God is highly exalted. Both horse and driver God has hurled into the sea." Could Miriam be, for us, a source of courage and bravery?
- *Remember Esther?* She used her position in authority to help others like her. Are we called to do the same?

- *Remember Hagar?* She becomes many things to many people, and one of the first females in scripture to experience use, abuse, and rejection. Yet her love for God knew no bounds.
- *Remember the nameless woman at the well?* Jesus revealed to her all of the good things she had done, and she became an evangelist. Could this nameless woman be for us the model of what we are called to be—a messenger, an evangelist?
- *Remember the bent-over woman?* Women need, especially in their conversation with other women, to lift each other up and not tear each other down. There is enough of that going on in the world and in our society. Women need to encourage other women. Let us do the same.
- *Remember the Canaanite woman?* She teaches us never to give up asking God for what we need.
- *Remember Mary of Magdala?* She can be remembered as the first of the apostles, the one who did not abandon Jesus at the cross—who was faithful despite the consequences. What about our own call to fidelity?

And of course, *remember Blessed Virgin Mary*. Her life will always be a model for us of fidelity and courage. Always remember to turn to her in time of need.

Perhaps we could choose a different woman from the scriptures each month—read their stories, practice their virtues, and listen closely to the message they give to us as we try to emulate and follow their example.

5. Don't allow yourself to be treated as an "afterthought."

There are often times when women do not stand up for themselves because they believe they don't matter. If you are one of these women, please don't allow others to treat you as an afterthought or as something added later, like an addition that was not included in the original plan. Do not allow others to define you as weaker, less important, or less valuable. You are the original plan. And as Daniel Berrigan once said: "Know where you stand, and stand there."

6. *Refuse to be cynical.*

Don't allow cynicism to take over your belief system. Cynicism suggests a disbelief in the sincerity of human motives. Cynicism leads to nothing good. It doesn't help anyone. Conan O'Brien was quoted as saying:

> All I ask is one thing, please don't be cynical. I hate cynicism, for the record, it's my least favorite quality and it doesn't lead anywhere. Nobody in life gets exactly what they thought they were going to get. But if you work really hard and you're kind, amazing things will happen.

I think Conan has it right. The church and our world need the people of God to embrace more outstanding and courageous qualities, such as forgiveness, kindness, goodness, and truth.

7. *Just because the church says no, doesn't mean that women can't say **yes**.*

The world needs bravery. Our world and our church needs women to be brave. Women cannot allow others to define them as weaker, less important, and less valuable. And as stated earlier, women are already there—they have not let others convince them that they have nothing to offer. They already work hard, work tirelessly and fearlessly. They don't run from challenge or danger. Women need not give up but are called to go to places where they are needed and places where Jesus leads them, despite the difficulties and fears.

Remember, we are all God's handiwork—God's treasure. Don't allow anyone to treat you as less than this. And on the other side of the coin—treat others the way you wish to be treated. If you are God's handiwork, so is the person sitting next to you—in the classroom, in the workplace, at the supper table. Believe in yourself, and believe in the goodness of the other. We, together, are a piece of God's finest tapestry, God's finest artwork—and in an age when everything, even life, is disposable, we need a sign. We need to see people who still care for one another in a world gone crazy. We need to believe and profess and act as if we are treasures of God and life is sacred or Christianity will itself become extinct.

And in conclusion, if we fail at being our best selves, or if we are not invited to the banquet, that doesn't mean we give up. It simply means that tomorrow is another day. And tomorrow, we try again, with God's grace. It is God who has the final answer, and in the end, it is God who does the inviting. God has already extended the invitation to women and men alike. No one is excluded from the banquet. Let us remember that it is God who has the last word, and in God we trust, because …

God knows us.

God sees us.

God calls us by our name.

We are God's beloved—male and female alike. And nothing and no one can take that away

What more is there to say!

ENDNOTES

1   "Simple Definition of Patriarchy," Merriam Webster Dictionary, accessed September 2, 2016, http://www.merriam-webster.com/dictionary/patriarchy.

2   *Analysis of the Art of Renaissance Italy, Michelangelo's Creation of Adam,* accessed July 8, 2016, http://www.italianrenaissance.org/michelangelo-creation-of-adam.

3   *Children and Young People's Drawings of God,* WebCite, accessed June 20, 2016, Children's and Young People's Drawings of God. 2012-05-11.

4   Ibid.

5   Ibid.

6   *Greek Philosophy on the Inferiority of Women,* accessed on June 10, 2016, www.womenpriests.org/traditio/inferior.asp.

7   Tertullian, *De cultu feminarum* (The Dress of Women), in *Corpus Christianorum, Series Latina,* volume 1 (Turnholt: Typographia Brepols, 1954), 343.

8   Elizabeth Johnson, *Consider Jesus, Waves of Renewal in Christology* (New York: Crossroads Publishing, 1996), 101.

9   Wijngaards Institute for Catholic Research, "*Women Can be Priests,*" accessed March 12, 2016, http://www.womenpriests.org/traditio/sinful.asp.

10   Council of Constantinople.

11   Henricus de Sergusio, *Commentaria in Quinque Decretalium Libros* in 1268, "Eighteen Reasons why women are worse off than men," translation from the Latin by John Wijngaards.

12   *Catechism of the Catholic Church* (New York: Catholic Book Publishing, 1994), 370.

13   "Simple Definition of Patriarchy," Merriam Webster Dictionary.

14   *"Patriarchal Worldview"* accessed March 2, 2016, http//encyclopedia2. thefreedictionary.com/Patriarchal worldview.

15   *"Plato and Aristotle on Women: Selected Quotes,"* About Education, philosophy.about.com/od/Philosophical-quotes-and-Lines/aPlataccessed March 21, 2016, http.

16   Ibid.

17   Ibid.

18   Women are defective males, "What the church says about women", accessed 2011, http://www.womenaredefectivemales.com/ what-the-church-says-about-women.

19   Ibid.

20   Elizabeth Johnson, *She Who Is* (New York: Crossroads Publishing, 1994), 24.

21   SermonCentral, "A Little Girl was drawing a picture of God," accessed September 2, 2016, http://www.sermoncentral.com/illustrations/sermon-illustration-ed-wood-humor-godthefather-21166.asp.

22   , The BLB Blog, "The Names of God: Adonai," accessed July 12, 2016, http:// blogs.blueletterbible.org/blb/2012/07/13/the-names-of-god-adonai.

23   http://www.gotquestions.org/Lord-is-my-shepherd.htmalQuestion.

24   Sallie McFague, *Models of God* (Philadelphia; Fortress Press, 1987), 106.

25   *Feminism and Christianity*, 65.

26   Regina A. Coll, *Christianity and Feminism in Conversation* (New London, CT: Twenty-Third Publications, 1998), 41.

27   John Paul I, Angelus, September 10, 1978,http://w2.vatican.va/content/ john-paul-i/en/angelus/documents/hf_jp-i_ang_10091978.html.

28   Catholic News Agency, "Even More, God is our Mother," Accessed January 07, 2014, written by Cheryl Dickow.

29   Time, "Why God is a Mother too," May 11, 2013, written by Yolanda Pierce, http://ideas.time.com/2013/05/11/why-god-is-a-mother-too.

30   A God-Man in Christ, *"Drinking of God as the Fountain of Living Waters to become His increase,"* accessed September 21, 2016, http://www.agodman. com/blog/drinking-of-god-as-the-fountain-of-living-waters-to-become-his-increase.

31   Wijngaards Institute for Catholic Research, *"The Holy Spirit as Feminine in Early Syriac Literature,"* Sebastian Brock. First Published as chapter 5, "After Eve," edited by Janet Marshall Soskice, Collins Marshall Pickering, 1990.

32   Ibid.

33   Catholic News Agency, Cheryl Dickow.

34 John Gillespie Magee Jr., accessed December 30, 2016, https://en.wikipedia.org/wiki/John_Gillespie_Magee,_Jr.

35 R. Hugh Connolly, http://www.bombaxo.com/Didascalia.html "Didascalia Apostolorum," Oxford: Clarendon Press, 1929, retrieved on 18 July 2013.

36 Bible tools, "*The Meaning of Divorce in the Old Testament in the Bible,* accessed January 7, 2015, http://www.bibletools.org/index.cfm/fuseaction/Def.show/RTD/ISBE/ID/2755/Divorce-in-Old-Testament.htm.

37 Women in the Scriptures, "Deborah," accessed June 17, 2009, http://www.womeninthescriptures.com/2009/06/deborah.html.

38 Future Church, "Women in the Bible and Lectionary by Ruth Fox, OSB," accessed January 5, 2015, https://www.futurechurch.org/women-in-church-leadership/women-and-word/women-in-bible-and-lectionary-by-ruth-fox-osb.

39 Ibid.

40 Peeling a Pomegranate, *Miriam the Prophetess, the Midrash,* accessed June 12, 2016, http://www.peelapom.com/spirituality/spiritual-practices/miriam-the-prophetess-a-midrash.

41 Treble, *Texts of Terror*, 5.

42 Patriarchal worldview.

43 *Saint Photini, the Samaritan Women,* http://www.orthodoxchristian.info/pages/photini.htm, Adapted from *Saints and Sisterhood: The lives of forty-eight Holy Women* by Eva Catafygiotu Topping, Light and Life Publishing Company.

44 Coll, *Christianity and Feminism in Conversation,* 165.

45 Ibid.

46 Mary Ann Getty-Sullivan, *Women in the New Testament* (Collegeville, MN: Liturgical Press, 2001), 80.

47 Anthony Gittins, *Encountering Jesus* (Liguiori, MO: Liguori Publications, 2002), 27.

48 Bible People, *Mary Magdalene, The Gospel Story,* accessed June 12, 2015, http://www.bible-people.info/Mary_Magdalene.htm.

49 Coll, *Christianity and Feminism in Conversation,* 163.

50 Sally Moran, *Women of the Covenant* (Bloomington, IN: First Books, 2003), 50.

51 Bible Odyssey, *"Mary Magdalene in Popular Culture"*, accessed January 3, 2016, http://www.bibleodyssey.org/en/people/related-articles/mary-magdalene-in-popular-culture.aspx

52   Catechism of the Catholic Church (New York: Catholic Book Publishing, 1994), 394.

53   *Catechism*, 1577.

54   L'Osservatore Romano, *Apostle of the Apostles (Apostolorum Apostola), June 10, 2016.*

55   Ibid.

56   Wikipedia, *The Liturgy of St. Basil,* accessed June 8, 2016, https://en.wikipedia.org/wiki/liturgy-of-Saint-Basil.

57   New Advent, *The Apostolic Constitutions, Book VIII,* accessed June 14, 2016, http://www.newadvent.org/fathers/07158.htm.

58   Women in the Bible, *"Mary of Magdalene at the Resurrection",* accessed July 2, 2015, www.womeninthebible.net/women-bible-women/mary-magdalene.

59   *The Council of Ephesus,* Catholic Encyclopedia, accessed November 1, 2016, http://www.newadvent.org/cathen/05491a.htm.

60   *In Search of the Real Mary,* Catholic Update, published by St. Anthony Messenger Press, article written by Elizabeth Johnson, March 20, 2001.

61   *Marialis Cultus,* # 37; February 2, 1974, accessed September 2, 2016, http://www.ewtn.com/library/PAPALDOC/P6MARIAL.HTM.

62   Ibid.

63   Mary Ann Getty-Sullivan, *Women in the New Testament* (Collegeville, MN: Liturgical Press, 2001), 255.

64   Our Catholic Faith, Ordinary time, Index to Saints, accessed October 5, 2015, http://www.ourcatholicfaith.org/saints/a.html.

65   *The Process of Beatification & Canonization,* accessed September 4, 2016, https://www.ewtn.com/johnpaul2/cause/process.asp.

66   Ibid.

67   Pope John Paul II, Apostolic Letter, *Mulieris Dignitatem,* #16, 1988, accessed June 20, 2016, http://w2.vatican.va/content/john-paul-ii/en/apost_letters/1988/documents/hf_jp-ii_apl_19880815_mulieris-dignitatem.html.

68   Before the Marian prayer, Pope Francis announced that on October 7, 2013, at the start of the ordinary Assembly of the Synod of Bishops, he will proclaim St. John of Avila and St. Hildegarde of Bingen as Doctors of the Universal Church.

69   *Feminine Martyrs in the Early Church,* accessed September 4, 2015, http://mariannedorman.homestead.com/femalemartyrs.html.

70   Roman Britain, The Annals, *Book XIII.xxii—The Trial of Pomponia Graecina the Wife of Aulus Plautius,* accessed June 12, 2016, http://roman-britain.co.uk/books/tacitus-annals.htm.

71   Early Christian Writings, *Pliny the Younger and Trajan on the Christians,* accessed September 2, 2015, http://www.religion.ucsb.edu/faculty/thomas/classes/rgst116b/Pliny.pdf.

72   History's Women, *Blandina, Slave Girl of Lyons,* accessed February 2, 2016, http://historyswomen.com/womenoffaith/Blandina.htm.

73   Wikipedia, *Thecla,* accessed September, 4, 2015, https://en.wikipedia.org/wiki/Thecla.

74   The St. Nina Quarterly, *Saint Nino and the Role of Women in the Evangelization of the Georgians,* accessed November 5, 2015, http://stnina.org/st-nina/her-life/st-nino-and-role-women-evangelization-georgians.

76   About Catholics, *Matthew, the Gospel of the Church,* accessed September 17, 2016, http://www.aboutcatholics.com/beliefs/matthew-the-gospel-of-the-church.

77   The Apostolic Tradition of Hippolytus, accessed September 5, 2015 www.rore-sanctifica.org/bibilotheque_rore_sanctifica/12.

78   Miriam- Webster dictionary, *Laity, accessed September 6, 2015,* http://www.merriam-webster.com/dictionary/laity.

79   Encyclopedia Britannica, *The Council of Nicaea,* accessed September 20 2015, https://www.britannica.com/event/Council-of-Nicaea-Christianity-325.

80   New Advent, *Apostolic Constitutions, accessed September 21, 2015,* http://www.newadvent.org/fathers/07158.htm.

81   Roger Gryson, *The Ministry of Women in the Early Church* (Collegeville, MN: Liturgical Press, 1976), 48–49.

82   New Advent, *Council of Chalcedon, accessed September 22, 2015,* http://www.newadvent.org/cathen/03555a.htm.

83   The Wijngaards Institute for Catholic Research, accessed September 22, 2015, *The Second Council of Orleans,* http://www.womenpriests.org/minwest/can_orl2.asp.

84   Catholic Women Deacons, *Women Deacons in Scripture, accessed September 22, 2015,* http://catholicwomendeacons.org/explore/explore-historydetails.

85   Aimee Georges Martimort, *Deaconesses; An Historical Study,* trans. K. D. Whitehead (San Francisco, CA: Ignatius Press, 1986), 38–39.

86   Cipriano Vagaggini, *"L'ordinazione delle diaconesse nella tradizione greca e bizantina,"* Orientalia christiana periodica 40 *(1974)* 151.

87   Vagaggini, 176.

88   Encyclopedia Britannica, *Gratians' Decretum,* accessed September 22, 2015, https://www.britannica.com/topic/Gratians-Decretum.

89   Ibid.

90   Corpus Iuris Canonici (all quotes from *Abbe Andre, Droit Canon,* P Ignatius Paris, 1859, volume 2, column 75).

91   Report of an Ad Hoc Committee of the Canon Law Society of America, *"The Canonical Implications of Ordaining Women to the Permanent Diaconate,"* published by the Canon Law Society of America, 1995.

92   History, Art and Archives, *The Women's Rights Movements, 1848- 1929,* accessed January 2, 2016, http://history.house.gov/Exhibitions-and-Publications/WIC/Historical-Essays/No-Lady/Womens-Rights.

93   Ruth L. O'Halloran, *The National Council of Catholic Women: The First 75 Years* (Washington, D.C.: National Council of Catholic Women, 2005), 6.

94   Ibid., 1.

95   Ibid., 6.

96   Vehementer Nos, accessed February 12, 2016, http://www.papalencyclicals.net/Pius10/p10law.htm.

97   Kenneth Briggs, *Double-Crossed,* (New York: Doubleday, 2006), 67.

98   Ibid., 70.

99   Ibid., 71.

100   May Luke Tobin, S.L., *Hope is an Open Door* (Nashville, TN: Abingdon, 1981), 30.

101   Carmel McEnroy, *Guests in their Own House: the Women of Vatican II* (Eugene, OR: Wipf and Stock Publishing, 1996), 72.

102   Briggs, 72.

103   Pope Paul VI, Constitution on the Church in the Modern World, *Gaudium et Spes,* December 7, 1965.

104   Ibid., #929.

105   Lumen Gentium.

106   *Sharon Euart article*

107   Rene Van Eyden, *"The Place of Women in Liturgical Functions,"* in *Concilium,* 4 1968, 75.

108   Katherine Meagher, S.C. *"Women in relation to orders and jurisdiction,"* edited by James Coriden, *Sexism and Church Law,* Paulist Press, 1977, 27.

109   Ibid., 75.

110   Ibid.

[111] Stanislaus Woywod, ed. *A Practical Commentary on the Code of Canon Law* (New York, Joseph F. Wagner, Inc. 1957), 587.
[112] Raoul Nax, ed. *Traite de Droit Canonique*, III, 230.
[113] Yves Congar, *Lay People in the Church* (Westminster, MD: Newman Press, 1965), 284.